INVESTING IN POTTERY & PORCELAIN

D1148994

INVESTING
IN

POTTERY & PORCELAIN
Hugo Morley~Fletcher

Transworld Publishers Ltd
a National General Company

INVESTING IN POTTERY AND PORCELAIN
A Corgi Book 0552 98535 X
Originally published in Great Britain by Barrie & Rockliff, The Cresset Press,
2 Clement's Inn, Strand, London, W.C.2
Text set by Yendall & Co., Ltd., London, E.C.4
Colour pages printed by L. Van Leer & Co. N.V. of Amsterdam
Text and Covers printed in Great Britain by Jarrold & Sons Ltd., Cowgate,
Norwich
Printing History
Barrie & Rockliff Edition published 1968
Corgi Edition published 1970
Copyright © Design Year Book Limited 1968
Corgi Books are published by Transworld Publishers Ltd., Cavendish House,
57–59 Uxbridge Road, London, W.5

Colour photography by Michael Plomer (pages 18 lower, 71, 72, 107 lower
left) and A. C. Cooper Ltd (pages 17, 35 top, 36 top, 89, 90, 107 top, 108,
126, 143, 144).

CONTENTS

INTRODUCTION

Collecting porcelain is no new idea in the English speaking world. In fact by the time that the first porcelain was produced in England Oriental porcelain had been arriving in Europe for a century and a half. This had recently been forced to compete with the products of Meissen and the early French factories. As a result the early porcelain manufacturers had a ready made and enthusiastic public for their wares. Pottery is a subject closer to the grass roots. The methods and techniques are mainly local to Staffordshire, though the delftwares belong to the European mainstream of tin glazed earthenwares.

The decoration and shapes come from a wide variety of sources; Japan, China, Germany, Holland, all contribute their differing and yet mingled influences while the impact of contemporary silver on both porcelain and pottery is fundamental and lasting. The mixture of all these differing ingredients produced wares and figures which, despite their undeniable Continental or Oriental antecedents, were nonetheless undeniably English.

Sprimont, Wedgwood, Duesbury, Littler, Champion and all the other great manufacturers catered for a collectors market. The collectors however did not seek an investment apart from the return in pleasure which possession of fine porcelain and pottery gave. Recent years may seem to have altered this picture. To the world of ceramics, as elsewhere in the arts, there has come the investment-collector. This has not however changed the fundamental facts. You cannot build a good collection without love for what you collect, knowledge brought by that love and constant contact with a wide variety of specimens. Thus it will always remain true that the most successful collectors are the most knowledgeable and it is their collections that will provide the most effective investment. Even where material return seems large, the invisible return is immeasurably greater.

Most people with any expert pretensions whatever have visions of making great contributions to scholarship. I must confess to being no exception to this rule: but the specialist textbook is not produced overnight, it is the distillation of years of experience and finds its place more in the reference library than on the ordinary bookshelf. The purpose of this book is entirely different. It does not attempt to break new ground in the facts that it presents, but only in the manner of their presentation. It does not set out to enumerate the minutiae of the history of the production of porcelain and pottery in England but to draw attention to the wide scope it offers to would be collectors. You will not therefore find in these pages precise biographical details of the potters discussed. Nor is there much reference to the business aspects of pottery and porcelain manufacture which are meat and drink to the specialist writer. If you wish to read the correspondence of Josiah Wedgwood or the details of the partnership at Chelsea, you must turn to specialist works on the subject. Similarly, although the mark, if any, on each illustrated specimen is described, there is no place in this book for detailed examination of the varied marks that are used. These should anyway serve only to confirm an attribution based on other more important criteria such as the paste, the form and the decoration, and are much better studied in books devoted to marks.

The prices attached to the specimens illustrated are generally the most recent realised *at auction*. When the piece shown changed hands some time ago the price has the date in brackets beside it. In several cases it has been possible to record a series of prices covering a number of years, thus showing trends more clearly. The illustrations in colour tend to represent the most expensive pieces, the English porcelain collector's equivalent to Paul de Lamerie, Stubbs and Chippendale. The majority of these are within the reach of only a few. The halftone illustrations include items worth from about £20 $50 upwards. They are naturally not exhaustive as not every aspect of the subject can be represented.

The division of the various chapters is governed by the normal trends of collecting. Thus the products of Josiah Wedgwood are separated from the 18th century potteries in Staffordshire of which they form a section. This is because Wedgwood has a strong specialist appeal of its own. Similarly because most collectors of figures pay little attention to wares from the same factories, and vice versa, the wares of Chelsea and Bow are separated from the figures.

Elsewhere, where the volume or variety of the manufactures does not justify ampler treatment, they are discussed together.

That this book is a book at all is due to the efforts, direct and indirect of many people. Thanks are due first to my wife both for typing the manuscript so beautifully and for putting up with the inconvenience of manuscript and photographs in an already crowded flat. Second to Antony du Boulay, who introduced me to English porcelain some five years ago. Among those who lent me photographic material and allowed pieces in their possession to appear are Mr. Robert Williams, Mr. & Mrs. Dwight M. Beeson, Mr. Peter Wilman, Mr. John Southern, Mrs. Kathleen Tilley and Mr. Christopher Elwes, to all of whom I am extremely grateful. Last thanks, but not least to Malcolm Davidson for his considerable advice, and to my publishers for their courage and their tolerance.

Three figures of the Turk's Companion.
Left
The Meissen original modelled by J. J. Kändler and P. Reinicke. Blue Crossed Swords mark at back.
Centre
A Bow example. Anchor and Dagger mark in red.
Right
A Chelsea example. Red Anchor mark.

Throughout this book British prices have been converted into United States dollars at the rate of $2.80 to the £ in the cases where they were quoted or paid previous to the devaluation of the Pound Sterling on 18th November, 1967. Subsequent prices have been converted at the present (1968) average rate of $2.40 to the £.

DELFTWARE

In Italy in the 15th and subsequent centuries there was developed and produced a fine tin-glazed earthenware. This, which became eventually highly sophisticated, was generally known as *maiolica*. The word maiolica itself was a corruption of Majorca, whence the ware was, wrongly, thought to originate. Tin-glazed earthenware was, in fact, developed in the Moorish part of the Spanish mainland. In France the same ware, when it arrived there in the 17th century, was known as *faience*, a transliteration of Faenza, one of the major centres of the production of Italian maiolica, while in Holland it was produced from the late 16th century and took its name from the principal centre of its production, the city of Delft. Germany too produced tin-glazed earthenware, or *fayence*, at a variety of centres.

England produced the tin that formed the glaze on the wares of all these countries and from the late 16th century tin-glazed earthenware was made in London. This continued during the 17th century and expanded to Bristol, Wincanton, Liverpool and other lesser centres around 1700. Its production continued till about 1800. The name by which pieces of this type are described is ' Delftware ', another anomaly in the true tradition of tin-glazed pottery. This is particularly strange since it is extremely likely that this country copied the Italians first. However, many of the workmen who were employed in the London delft factories in the 17th century were Dutch and the use of the word dates only from about 1700.

Examples of the earliest known pieces of delft ware, such as the Malling jugs with their contemporary silver mounts, are so rare that they are within the reach of museums and a few wealthy collectors only. However, pieces

Octagonal blue and white 'Merry Man' plate. Lambeth *circa* 1670. The thick, creamy appearance of this is typical of the very early blue and white wares. This is the fourth of a series of eight plates, each bearing a phrase from the poem:

What is a merry man
Let him do what he can
To entertain his guests
With wine and merry jests
But if his wife doth frown
All merriment goes down.

The spelling, as on this plate, is varied and sometimes odd even by 17th century standards.

A complete set of these plates is probably worth almost £2,000, $4,800 today, though a single specimen could be found for under £100, $240.

7¾ in. diameter.

A blue and white dated plate: Lambeth 1698. Dated pieces are particularly valued because they help to place similar but undated specimens in context. This plate is rather more thinly potted than the Merry Man example of twenty years earlier. This elaborate type of cartouche is to be found round a variety of inscriptions, initials or dates.

£70, $170.

10¼ in. diameter.

A Lambeth delft Claret Jug dated 1646. The inscription is in underglaze blue.

6¼ in. high.

12

A Lambeth delft Sack Jug dated 1646. Sack or sherry was a very popular 17th century drink.

A good plain example such as this might fetch up to £150, $360 today.

6¼ in. high.

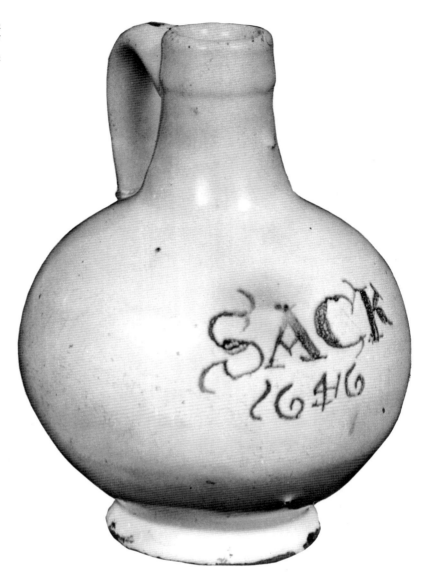

were made in the 17th century which, although increasing in value, are more widely obtainable. London was the principal manufacturing centre during this period. The wares made during the first half of the century are notable for their whiteness and for their simple decoration in blue. Typical of these are the amusing bottles for wine, which are often painted with the name of the contents; ' Claret ' or ' Sack ', above a date. It is not known precisely whether the date records the vintage, or the date of bottling. Another suggestion which is quite plausible is that these bottles were given, full, as Christmas presents. Either way they are an extremely homely record of the drinking habits of the age. As in Italy and Holland, jars were also made for Apothecaries, who needed cylindrical jars for powders and ewers for liquids. These were generally named on the outside in blue. The name was enclosed in a frame or cartouche in scroll or strapwork form, often with cherubs' heads, perched birds and vases of flowers. The form of the frames changed with contemporary fashions in art, and collectors have concentrated on documenting the various types and different drugs whose names are to be found on the jars.

The products for which the 17th century delft factories are most renowned are the ' blue dash ' chargers which were made between 1640 and about 1700. In 16th century Italy the majority of the highly decorated maiolica dishes

13

were made not to eat off but to hang on the wall or to place on the sideboard.
They appear in contemporary paintings fulfilling exactly this purpose.
English delft chargers too are often pierced for hanging on the wall. They
afforded many of the decorative qualities of paintings and were, of course, much
cheaper. They are known as 'blue dash' chargers because they frequently
have blue splashes all round their rims. The most famous dishes of this type
are the Royal Portrait Chargers. These begin with Charles I, who is depicted
standing, crowned and robed. His son, Charles II, appears in much the same
guise, whilst James II and William III are shown on horseback. Other
figures who are found on chargers are Marlborough, Prince Eugene, and the
Duke of Ormonde. These dishes too are of fine quality. This alas does not
apply to those of George I and II, who appear rarely on chargers, since
they were never really popular among the ordinary people of their adopted
kingdom. Furthermore, they appeared at the very end of the era when most
of the originality and zest had gone out of the production.

Charles II dated portrait charger. This is
modelled on similar chargers depicting
Charles I, of which the most outstanding
example is at Chequers in Buckinghamshire.
Specimens in good condition are very rare
today.
16¼ in. diameter.

Next in importance after portrait chargers are those representing 'The Fall
of Man' and known as Adam and Eve Chargers. These may have been
prompted by the Puritan preoccupation with Sin; at the same time it is
amusing to note that the fruit on the tree is generally represented as oranges,
perhaps a topical reference to William III. It may also have been popular
to offer people fruit from a dish depicting 'man's first disobedience and the
fruit of the forbidden tree'. A more common, but much more varied type

of charger is that known as the 'tulip charger'. This type has a symmetrical arrangement of flowers, in which tulips often predominate, growing from grassy mounds or in baskets or vases. Although fundamentally the same, these chargers display an infinite variety of colours, floral forms and patterns and are at least as desirable as Adam and Eve chargers. Other varieties occur with a pattern of oak leaves and are therefore called oak leaf chargers. Some are also found with formal designs, which are unusual but lack the strong decorative qualities of the other types. Care should be taken to distinguish these from the extremely similar dishes, more thickly potted, which were made in France at the beginning of the last century. Although these chargers all have strong family likenesses, it is not yet certain whether they were made exclusively in London or whether some of them derive from the Brislington factory near Bristol. The issue is further confused by the fact that workmen from Southwark were employed to establish the Brislington factory.

For the beginner, the problem of distinction between the four major

Blue dash tulip charger: London *circa* 1680. The decoration is in ochre and other fairly sombre tones. The formal arrangement of the tulips and carnations is derived from Isnik or Rhodian pottery of the 16th and early 17th centuries. These are probably the most common type of charger, but there are wide varieties to be found.
In 1960 £50, $140, in 1968 £120, $290. 13¼ in. diameter.

factories of the 18th century is perplexing. Lambeth and Bristol, Liverpool and Wincanton all produced wares painted in underglaze blue as well as polychrome or coloured wares, and the themes that appear on the products of all these factories are basically the same. The blue and white of Bristol, Lambeth and Liverpool derive their themes from the same sources but interpret them in markedly different ways. The very colour of the blue, although the basic cobalt colouring was always the same, varies from one

Blue dash oak leaf charger: London *circa* 1680. A rarer type than the tulip charger but less obviously decorative. This example is painted in an unusually pale turquoise, yellow and blue palette.
£120, $290.
13 in. diameter.

Blue dash equestrian charger: London or Bristol *circa* 1688. The horseman, who is holding a Commander's baton, could represent either James II or William III, entirely according to the loyalties of the owner. Thus the potters assured themselves of a good market in a world of conflicting and changing sympathies.
£250, $600.
14 in. diameter.

Opposite page

A Worcester fluted teapot and cover with Giles decoration. Blue Square Seal mark. The superb ciselé gilding is similar to that on the Chelsea claret ground dish. This pattern can be also identified in the Giles sale of 1774.
This teapot sold in 1968 for £525, $1,260. A similar one in 1957 fetched £57, $140.

A Worcester pink scale and hop trellis teapot and stand. It is extremely rare today to find Worcester teapots of this period still united with their stands. This example has the further advantage of a desirable pink border with the hop trellis design, which is one of the factory's most popular patterns. Hop trellis patterns also occur with turquoise and royal blue borders.

Over page

A Staffordshire saltglaze teapot and cover—this is an unusual example since it combines relief and enamel decoration. The reliefs themselves are out of the normal run and it is probable that the teapot is connected with some martial event in the 1740's.
Colonial Williamsburg

A Whieldon solid agate coffee pot and salver. The predecessor of Wedgwood's similar wares. Here again the shape owes much to the silversmith. The salver is little different in shape from its silver contemporary, but as a piece of pottery it is extremely sophisticated.

factory to the next. This variation is caused in part by the different nature of the actual white surface, which is pinker and softer at Lambeth and harder and bluer at Bristol. The blue painted areas on Liverpool pieces tend to sink below the remaining surface, whilst Bristol presents a hard and even surface overall. The Lambeth surface is softer than Bristol, more so even than Liverpool.

An interesting sideline in the decoration of blue and white pieces is derived from Italian 16th century maiolica. This is the technique known as *bianco-sopra-bianco* in which white enamel is painted on a white ground. In fact, the enamel is always whiter than the white glazed surface of the delft. Wares of this type were produced at Bristol, Lambeth and Liverpool, with *bianco-sopra-bianco* borders and blue and white central fields. The decoration of the borders from all these factories is similar, but most successful on Bristol pieces where the very hard surface supports the enamel better than the softer wares of Lambeth and Liverpool. On these the enamel tends to sink in and lose contrast. The decorative themes of the borders at all the factories are

An Adam and Eve charger: Bristol *circa* 1710. The sponged effect round the rim shows that this is a late example of the type. Earlier 'Fall' dishes have the blue dash rims apparent on the other types. Blue predominates in the palette. Here the colours are more varied while the sponging is more typical of Bristol than Lambeth, though Adam and Eve chargers were made at both centres.
£150, $360.
12¾ in. diameter.

OPIFERQUE PER.ORBEM .DICOR.

fundamentally the same, embodying pineapples, pinecones and leaf scrolls.

Polychrome wares derive their inspiration from the same sources. Many of them display a liberal interpretation of Chinese themes. Others are painted with flower sprays or commemorative subjects. Chinese blue and white porcelain was arriving in this country throughout the 18th century. This provided the most common inspiration for the decorators of the blue and white wares. Sometimes, as in the case of the Liverpool vase illustrated, the relationship between Chinese originals and the delft interpretation is fairly direct and obvious.

20

A blue and white pill slab with the arms of the Apothecaries' Company: Liverpool *circa* 1720. These slabs, which are to be found in a variety of forms, oval, heart-shaped and others, were made in London and Liverpool. They were displayed on the wall outside chemists' shops. They may also have been used for rolling pills. The pill slab has always been keenly sought after by delft collectors.

£500, $1,200.

10¾ in. high.

In other cases Chinese figures are shown in markedly English surroundings, or there are incongruous combinations of Western themes with Chinese decorative motifs such as borders of lotus or ju-i pattern. Another source of ideas was the vast volume of Dutch delft wares produced at this time. So close is the adherence to Dutch styles of decoration on occasions that it is difficult to be certain whether a piece is Dutch or English.

Other blue and white pieces are manifestly English in decoration. Both Bristol and Lambeth produced very attractive plates and bowls painted with pastoral scenes. These include some of the finest pieces of the period. In the past a whole series of Bristol plates with ' sponged ' trees and rather attenuated figures was attributed to a painter called Niglett. This attribution was made on rather tenuous grounds and is today disregarded by expert opinion. Some of the finer pieces of Bristol blue and white pastoral wares can with some certainty be attributed to a painter by the name of Bowen. Elections and other political subjects, such as the John Wilkes affair, came in for their share of comment from the delft potters. Liverpool, then as now a great port, specialised in bowls painted with ships and naval inscriptions. At Lambeth, towards the end of the period, Lunardi's ascent in a balloon was commemorated. Some of the most attractive of Bristol's productions are the so-called farmhouse

A Liverpool delft blue and white bottle: a very typical example of Liverpool decoration in the Oriental idiom.

A Lambeth delft blue and white bowl, *circa* 1700. The deep shape with almost vertical sides is typical of early 18th century English delftware. The formal decoration is inspired by contemporary Chinese porcelains.
£150, $360.
10¼ in.

A Lambeth delft polychrome bowl, *circa* 1710. The form is slightly shallower, and the decoration is a typical 'interpretation' of a Chinese original. This, though coloured, is less rare than the earlier blue and white piece.
£100, $240.
10¼ in.

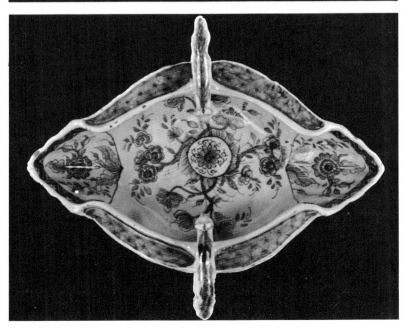

A Liverpool delft blue and white double-lipped sauce boat *circa* 1750. Shaped pieces of delft are extremely uncommon. This piece with its unusual fox handles is a very rare specimen. Double-lipped sauce boats are not easy to find in porcelain, though several were made at Worcester. However, many arrived from China and this example is, apart from the handles, a fairly faithful copy of one of these.
£150, $360.

plates, painted with different birds such as cocks, peacocks, and pheasants among sponged manganese trees. Liverpool produced plates with a delightful floral pattern known as 'Fazackerley'.

Although plates and dishes formed by far the greater part of the delft factories' production a large number of other types were also made. These include bowls such as the illustrated examples from Liverpool and Lambeth. The vases, mentioned before, are also to be found, while others were of different and more elaborate shapes. An exotic form that seems peculiar to English delft is the 'brick'. This is a plain rectangular object, with a pierced top, generally with several small holes surrounding a central large one. It is not certain what these were intended for, but it has been sugggested that they were inkwells, with the smaller holes to be used as quill-holders. An alternative idea is that they were used as bulb pots. These were made at all three of the major factories and are generally about six inches long. Larger examples, about 11 inches in length, are very much rarer. The majority of these bricks are blue and white: the more attractive ones are painted with chinoiserie scenes, the ordinary ones with flower sprays. Polychrome specimens are very much rarer, although some Bristol examples are occasionally to be found.

A Bristol delft blue and white brick, *circa* 1750. These bricks were made at Lambeth, Bristol and Liverpool. Most of them are blue and white although coloured ones were made at Bristol. Although they all are of the same shape, they may have fulfilled a variety of purposes, either as ink wells, the small holes holding numerous quills which were dipped in a large centre hole, or as bases for flower arrangements.

Up to 1965 these could be bought for £12–15 $30–36, but today one such as this would cost £30, $70 or more.

5¾ in. wide.

The early pieces of delft, the drug jars and sack or claret bottles from London, have always been collected. Similarly, the chargers, particularly those with Royal portraits of the Charles's, have always been very highly prized. In fact it is unlikely that such a charger, if it appeared on the market, would fetch less than £700–£800, $1700–$1900. Until now the other varieties of the 17th century charger, such as tulip and oak leaf dishes, were somewhat overshadowed by the portrait charger. As the majority of the early portrait chargers have now found their way into permanent collections and museums, collectors wanting chargers of blue dash type have been

23

A pair of Lambeth delft blue and white wall pockets *circa* 1740. Wall pockets occur in saltglaze and from various porcelain factories. This pair shows an amusing type of decoration in the Chinoiserie manner.
A pair might cost £250–300, $600–700, though a single example would bring less than half this.
8 in. high.

compelled to content themselves with tulip, oak leaf or Adam and Eve dishes. As a result these are now appreciating consistently.

The history of collecting 18th century delft is very different. The famous old collections, such as the Glaisher (now in the Fitzwilliam Museum), the Gautier (sold at the end of the war), the Garner (dispersed by Sotheby's 1964-65) and the Mellor (Christie's 1965, with the 17th century pieces now in the Victoria & Albert Museum) contained examples from both centuries, but in the first two of these the 18th century pieces were very lightly regarded. It is to Professor F.H. Garner that the current and increasing enthusiasm for 18th century wares is in great measure due. He not only formed an important collection, but in his book *English Delftware*, he made the first general attempt to distinguish between the major factories. His book made no claims to be, and was not, the last word on the subject, but it created an interest in delftware which seems daily stronger. Yet, by comparison with 17th century pieces, the products of the 18th century are not expensive. Despite the gathering interest very few dishes fetch as much as £50, $120, whilst apart

Three delft plates; left to right, Bristol polychrome with *Bianco-sopra-bianco* decoration.
Lambeth blue and white with oriental type decoration.
Lambeth with unusual blue and manganese decoration.
All these are pieces of good quality sold in 1965 for under £20, $50 each.

A Bristol polychrome plate, *circa* 1740. The red and yellow on this piece stand out distinctly from the glaze in a way typical of Bristol. The Chinaman in this curious attitude is also to be found on Dutch and German tinglazed earthenware.

This is a good example of the sort of plate that may still be acquired for under £30, $70.

from wall pockets, or rare dated or commemorative items, hardly any 18th century delftwares would cost more than twice that figure. Since contemporary porcelains of equivalent quality are much more expensive, many people are turning to delftwares and will certainly continue to be attracted by them. The most definite monetary appreciation will be found in the case of pieces of rare shape, such as teapots, mugs, sauceboats and bowls, which are always more difficult to find than flat pieces. Similarly, dated specimens will tend to be more sought after than undated ones of the same shape. In general, of course, blue and white pieces are less rare than polychrome examples: but all the above comments merely qualify the undoubtedly strong interest in a particularly fascinating aspect of English potting.

Three inscribed pieces of English delft.
Left to right:
Liverpool blue and white punch bowl, *circa* 1750.
Bristol electioneering plate decorated in manganese and blue and made for the Northampton election in 1759 at which Cresswell was returned to Parliament.
Bristol blue and white bowl with powdered manganese exterior.

Pottery in Staffordshire 1700-1830

The English delft manufacturers carried on a losing struggle against the rising tide of successful porcelain manufacture at home and abroad. The potters of Staffordshire, however, did not knuckle under so easily. They demonstrated throughout the golden age of porcelain the will and the ability to produce pottery that could compete with the greater sophistication of porcelain. The basic materials and the types of pottery used in Staffordshire did not change significantly during the 18th century. Although refinements were made, and the Industrial Revolution brought the capacity to produce quantity and quality, the wares of Josiah Wedgwood, who personifies the efficiency of the closing years of the century, do not differ fundamentally from the products of his predecessors around 1700.

The earliest products are slipwares: pottery of a reddish colour covered in dark glazes which are in turn decorated in pale glazes, generally of a yellowish tone. These are by no means common, and few if any pieces of this type are available to collectors. The foremost exponents of this type of ware were the Toft family who produced numerous dated and commemorative pieces. To see examples of these the student must visit the major public collections. The early wares that the collector might expect to acquire come from the potters of Astbury and men like Thomas Wedgwood, father of the better known Josiah. They produced red stonewares, (later to be dignified by Josiah Wedgwood with the name *Rosso Antico*), salt glazed stonewares, wares with applied slip decoration, and creamwares. The red wares, derived from or inspired by similar pieces produced in China, were developed by the Elers family. It was they who discovered that the material could be turned on a lathe, and who did away with the need for a glaze by making it non-porous by a second firing. More important than anything they actually produced was the impetus they gave to all their contemporaries to raise the standard of their products.

A scratch blue saltglaze two handled cup. This ware with its incised blue decoration was developed by Enoch Booth in the 1740's. This piece, with its Jacobite inscription is a rare example, though more ordinary pieces are not hard to find.

An enamelled saltglaze teapot. An example of this type of ware with a European subject.

Astbury took the process one stage further by stamping designs on pads of white slip which were applied to the red ware body: the whole was then covered in a glaze which coloured the body a warm brown, while the slip, as in the earlier wares, turned cream. The same stamped patterns are to be found on a different type of ware: salt-glazed stoneware. This too was an old established type, for the Germans in the 15th century had discovered that the inclusion of salt in the kiln imparts a glaze to the surface of stonewares. The resulting substance was widely used for the wine bottles which began to arrive in this country during the Elizabethan era. These, like the stonewares made at Fulham by John Dwight, made heavy and fairly insensitive use of the material. The Staffordshire potters of the 1730's and 1740's produced wares which could hardly contrast more strongly with those of their predecessors.

The competition with porcelain, at first imported and subsequently indigenous, forced the Staffordshire potters to produce a ware of comparable fineness. They were also forced to make a much whiter, more sophisticated form of stoneware. It was possible to model this very finely, while the applied decorations, previously found on the red wares, are much sharper when imposed on a white saltglaze base. Although developed in the 1730's it was between 1740 and 1760 that salt-glazed wares were produced in the greatest quantities. Many of the pieces are white with a great variety of moulded or applied decoration. Large numbers of plates and dishes were made, with moulded scroll and basketwork patterns in innumerable combinations and permutations. Cups, teapots and mugs occur with many applied motifs. Other pieces have incised decoration, and others still, particularly jugs and teapots, are moulded in the form of Palladian mansions, grotesque animals and shells. Certain of these also occur with coloured decoration; but the majority of examples of coloured saltglaze are quite different from those with moulded motifs. A large body of wares exist with decoration in the *famille rose* style, for saltglaze ware lends itself very well to enamelled decoration. The pieces that were used as the vehicle for coloured decoration generally have plain bodies. The mugs are bell shaped, the coffee pots of plain spreading cylindrical form, the teapots simply rounded. Only the handles and spouts receive the interest of form. Generally these are what are called ' crabstock ' handles and spouts, resembling gnarled branches studded with numerous knots. Occasionally they are spotted in one of the major colours of the body.

29

Three Staffordshire saltglaze teapots. All these have decoration in the *famille rose* vernacular. The handles and finials, however, are of a typical crabstock form which is one of the hallmarks of Staffordshire potting between 1740 and 1770. A good example with Oriental decoration may cost £150, $360. Pieces with European decoration are rarer.

Most of these pieces are decorated in spirited Oriental style. Others, as in all pottery, make a commentary on contemporary events such as the 1745 Rising and the Seven Years' War. Teapots are to be found with kilted Scotsmen or with portraits of Frederick the Great. European subjects also appear, such as pastoral scenes and figures of ladies and gentlemen, while another small category are teapots covered in an even Littler's blue glaze.

Salt-glazed wares were produced by the majority of the Staffordshire factories, among them the partnership between Thomas Whieldon and the young Josiah Wedgwood, but a second staple product of the 1740's was solid agate ware. This was achieved from a mixture of different coloured clays which produced a marbled effect. The ware relied for its effect entirely on the varied colour of the body. Teapots and mugs are perhaps the most common, but other pieces, such as the salver shown, are found.

The solid agate ware continued well into the Wedgwood era, but it gradually lost ground to the marbled glazed creamwares which were developed by Thomas Whieldon and which are usually known by his name. These wares are substantially the ancestors of our modern earthenwares. Most of Whieldon's productions were splashed in manganese, green, yellow, brown and occasionally blue under the glaze. This gives to some of the pieces a tortoiseshell effect and they are often described as ' tortoiseshell ' wares. The majority of these are plates, with milled edges and octagonal form, teapots, sugar basins and other table pieces. Some are moulded with branches and surmounted by

Opposite page

A Staffordshire saltglaze coffee pot and cover. The decoration derives evidently from contemporary Chinese *famille rose* porcelain. The form, however, finds its source more in contemporary silver. The combination is something entirely original and very effective. This type of piece is not easily found, though teapots occur much more frequently than coffee pots.

bird finials which give an Oriental effect. Others of Whieldon's products were creamwares with simple decoration. In fact his lifetime saw the gradual change in emphasis from salt-glazed wares to the creamware which dominates the latter half of the century. Earliest among these may be the cauliflower moulded wares. These are generally found as teapots, coffee pots and tea caddies on which the leaves alone are simply decorated in green, the remaining cream coloured surface being left plain. Unfortunately, although Whieldon lived until 1795, and must undoubtedly have produced creamwares of the plain sort, nothing was actually marked by him and the only pieces that can be attributed to him with any degree of confidence are those resembling the shards excavated on the site of his factory at Fenton Low. It is only with his partner Josiah Wedgwood, who marked his pieces fairly regularly from about 1765, that we enter the realm of confident attribution. Wedgwood's output forms, as we shall see, a complete field on its own for the collector.

From about 1740 the potteries in Staffordshire saw an increasing output of figures, often at those same factories which produced the wares we have been discussing. Astbury would seem to have been one of the pioneers in this sphere and some of his horsemen, soldiers and other figures have long been justly prized. Other saltglaze manufacturers produced groups of musicians, The Fall, Pew groups and other subjects in which the limbs of the figures have a rather sausage-like appearance reminiscent of plasticine modelling. Pieces of this type are again extremely rare. Thomas Whieldon's tortoiseshell effects were not confined to tablewares. Among his most famous products are

A Staffordshire saltglaze white tureen and cover. Undecorated pieces of this type are at a disadvantage when compared with coloured pieces. Despite this they often reveal rather better the technical efficiency of the potters and the fine quality of the modelling.

A Sailorman toby jug: one of the variants on the Toby Jug theme. The palette of pale greens, yellow and brown is a particularly good one and typical of Ralph Wood's work.

A Ralph Wood St George and the Dragon group. The slightly speckled decoration dates this piece somewhat later than the Sailorman Toby illustrated and looks forward to the Pratt type at the end of the century.

Opposite page
An oval Worcester tureen stand, from the Duke of Gloucester service. Gold Crescent mark. A rare shape combined with the work of the Cut Fruit Painter at his best.
10 in. wide.
Left and right
Two Chelsea scent bottles. One a gardener with a boy, the other a carp caught in a net.
Centre
Two Chelsea bonbonnières, one modelled as goldfinches and their brood on a nest, the other as lovers embracing. Both with enamel covers from Battersea.

A Chelsea circular saucer dish. Red Anchor mark. A good example of the Hans Sloane type of decoration, this piece is unusual in that it depicts a fruiting specimen. The design is arranged very carefully within the shape of the dish.

In 1967 this fetched almost £1,000, $2,800, though more ordinary examples with plainer shapes can be bought for £300—400, $720—950.

Chinese water buffalos and other animals splashed in coloured glazes, among which brownish manganese dominates. These were inspired by Chinese porcelain birds and animals dating from the beginning of the century which were decorated by a comparable technique. But his contribution to the field of figure pottery is greatly exceeded by that of Ralph Wood the Elder.

Ralph Wood, the second of three potters of the same name who between them spanned the 18th century, produced a wide range of figures, animals and Toby Jugs. In this he was aided by the modeller Voyez who worked at several different factories in Staffordshire during his career. Ralph Wood's figures are always very thinly potted and generally splashed in green and manganese. These colours are applied much more sparsely than on Whieldon figures. The bases are generally hollow and the interiors unglazed. The figures, animals and groups usually stand on rockwork. Among the animals which Wood produced are squirrels, deer and foxes. His figures include classical gods and goddesses, shepherds and shepherdesses, while among his groups are to be found Hudibras, St. George slaying the dragon and The Duke of Cumberland on horseback, though the last is extremely rare.

Toby Jugs are a very special field in which Wood would seem to have been a pioneer. The majority of these jugs, inspired by an engraving of a famous toper from Yorkshire, are fairly standard variations on the theme: Sir Toby is usually represented in tricorne hat, holding a frothing jug of beer and a pipe or a glass. In these standard examples the only difference lies in the quality of the decoration. However, there are also a number of rarer types of jug which depict other personalities. Among these are Martha Gunn, the Brighton bathing machine attendant who served George IV when a boy; Prince Hal; The Planter; The Sailor; The Squire; and Lord Vernon. Most of these were figures associated in the public mind with lusty drinking. Ralph Wood's original success with Toby Jugs, and indeed other figures, was carried on by his son, the third of the name, known as Ralph Wood the Younger. The potting of his pieces is rather thicker and clumsier than his father's. The same models are still to be found, but raised on mounds and solid square bases. The decoration too is different. The soft manganese and green tones are replaced by orange, black, green and blue and by the addition of brighter colours borrowed from the porcelain manufacturers. The repertoire of subjects changes too. There is an increase of figures with religious associations derived from the Methodist preaching of John Wesley. Figures of Elijah and the Widow, the Vicar and Moses and the Evangelists all appealed to the current religious enthusiasm. Enoch Wood, who succeeded Ralph Wood the Younger as manager of the factory numbered among his finest products a bust of Wesley himself.

Enoch Wood subsequently went into partnership with Thomas Caldwell: they produced creamwares in the Regency taste and figures and busts in the established tradition. Among their original creations were extremely attractive small figures of lions painted in shades of brown and ochre. Neale of Hanley also produced numerous figures and Toby jugs during the 1750's. Superficially these are virtually indistinguishable from the products of Ralph Wood the Younger and Enoch Wood. However, Neale made a practice of marking his products, and his work can thus be recognised. Felix Pratt of Fenton, a potter working close to the Wood orbit, gave his name to a whole body of wares and figures either with sponged spotted decoration in various shades or moulded in relief and enriched in colour. Prominent among these are a group of jugs with portraits of Nelson and Hardy, scenes of Chaunticleer and the Fox and caricature subjects. Plaques also occur with similar reliefs decorated in bright colours. Stirrup cups are also found in this class. All the wares of this type can be extremely attractive.

Another potter who worked in the early 19th century was John Walton of Burslem. He produced brightly coloured and naïvely modelled figures and groups. These included pastoral subjects, and themes of religious interest such as were popular in the previous generation. They are often raised on high bases and have small stunted flowering trees. Frequently they have the name Walton impressed on a scroll at the back. Pastoral groups are comparatively common, but some of the religious ones, or those depicting unusual animals, are more difficult to find. Groups such as these have long been comparatively popular; but recently, in tune with the great interest in

Four rare Chelsea scent bottles modelled as fruit, with gold mounts.

figures from later in the century, collectors have begun to pursue the rarer models avidly. Only recently a group of the Raising of Lazarus fetched over £100, $240 at auction; but an average example of good quality can be bought for much less. Similarly, in the realm of Prattwares there has been a strong increase in interest of late. The moulded jugs of the Nelson and Hardy type fetch between £30 and £40, $70–$100 whilst an unusually fine specimen has fetched even more. Jugs moulded with less common subjects command correspondingly higher prices and will continue to do so. The same applies to the Pratt plaques, tea caddies and stirrup cups, all of which seem to benefit from the popularity of pottery of this date.

The products of Enoch Wood are also appreciating steadily in value. So too are those of the Ralph Woods, father and son. But here we come to an interesting point. Ralph Wood Toby Jugs were the objects of immense enthusiasm during the opening years of this century. During this period collectors competed keenly for the rarer examples. Several famous collections of Toby Jugs were then being formed. One of these, the Mackintosh Collection, recently came back on the market after nearly fifty years. It included a Martha Gunn Toby Jug which in 1917 established a world record price for a Toby Jug of 600 gns, $1,400. In 1967 it fetched £400, $1,000, a considerable loss. Probably, had the collection appeared on the market earlier, in the 1930's, 40's or 50's, the loss would have been even greater. The Toby Jug market is now probably rising fairly steadily, but it is not an easy one. The Mackintosh sale gave it a considerable shot in the arm but even so the market is less consistent than all the other forms of English pottery. This is partly because Toby Jugs have few variations: the rarest specimens apart, they tend to differ only marginally one from another. Even the finest specimens of the more ordinary models are difficult to sell, and therefore, while no collection of pottery can be complete without an example of Ralph Wood's Toby Jugs, it would be hazardous to invest a large sum in a collection of these pieces. With Ralph Wood's other figures, however, the story is very different. Their appeal has undergone the same cycle as that of Toby Jugs; but their

A Ralph Wood group of Hudibras. This group is one of Ralph Wood's most famous products. The present example is a latish one and dates probably from the 1780's. The dark colours are indicative of this.

Four Staffordshire figures:
    A Gardener – Ralph Wood.
    Winter – of Pratt type.
    Apollo – Ralph Wood and marked with his rebus, a tree.
    Flora – late Wood or early Pratt.
The Apollo, apart from the mark of Ralph Wood on it, stands out through the quality of its modelling and did in fact fetch more than the other figures together.

interest to collectors is much more universal. Therefore, in the current atmosphere of buoyancy, they are appreciating in value as evenly as any other wares.

The products of Whieldon and the young Wedgwood have recently benefited from much research and from the excavations at Fenton Low. As more and more is discovered about this period, collectors are able to buy pieces with greater certainty. There are, however, large numbers of specimens in circulation which bear a superficial resemblance to Whieldon's products, and these should be approached with great caution. Pieces of this sort often fetch 'gamblers prices' in auction sales or are offered by dealers at prices equivalent to half the normal for accepted pieces. This is a period where the provenance of the piece should be studied carefully and, where any doubt exists, it should be avoided. The salt-glazed pieces of the 1740's and 1750's are easier to deal with. The ordinary enamelled teapot with decoration in the *famille rose* style can still be acquired for less than £100, $240. Examples with European scenes are rarer and therefore more expensive. So too are commemorative pieces. Mugs and dishes and other rare forms are also likely to cost rather more, if indeed they can be found. Moulded saltglaze pieces, having no coloured decoration, were for a long time very cheap. The average moulded plate could be bought for only a few pounds. Recently they have shown a marked increase. Moulded baskets and more elaborate specimens, which are less common, are of course proportionately higher in price. Wares with applied reliefs are rarer than any of the plain moulded pieces, but when compared with the coloured pieces they are, because of their plain colour, less expensive. Groups in saltglaze however, are virtually impossible to find today. It is probable that only a very few were originally made and the examples that do appear on the market fetch prices in the thousands.

Astbury's groups and figures of soldiers are again almost unobtainable today. In 1965 an equestrian group with the horseman's arms entirely missing was sold for nearly £500, $1,200. Had it been a complete specimen it would certainly have brought much more. No other specimen of the type has recently appeared on the market, but were it to do so the price would be correspondingly very much higher. The teawares of Astbury are rare, but, despite this, not tremendously expensive, and it is probably true to say that the earlier products of the Staffordshire potteries are at present slightly undervalued in comparison with those dating from the end of the 18th century. This is partly to be explained by the steady flow of the later wares which have helped to form a healthy and competitive market. The earlier wares are almost too thinly spread to allow private collectors the opportunity to add to their collections as often as most of them would like.

A very rare Ralph Wood elephant and monkey teapot, probably intended even originally more as a decorative than a practical piece. This is splashed in pale green and yellow glazes.

41

WEDGWOOD

In the age of factories liable to financial vicissitudes and short lives, one man arose out of the Whieldon circle and created a household word. Josiah Wedgwood developed an entirely new form of ware, which has continued in production, in a debased fashion, to this day.

Josiah Wedgwood was born in 1730. His family were small potters in Burslem producing wares of all the varieties discussed in the last chapter. It was at the age of eleven that Josiah joined his brother at the Churchyard works. However, in 1752 he went into partnership with Whieldon at Fenton Low. Whieldon, as we have seen, was exceptional only in the quality of his products. Wedgwood remained with Whieldon for about six years and was then rich enough to set up on his own at The Ivy House, Burslem. Here he concentrated on the first of his major contributions to the development of pottery in this country. This was the improvement of creamware or *faience fine*. Hitherto this had been used by Whieldon and his contemporaries covered

A Wedgwood and Bentley black basalt library bust of Joseph Addison, marked Wedgwood and Bentley. The highly polished surface is typical of black basalt busts and vases of the first period. This and the absence of mould marks distinguishes the 18th century products from the many later examples that were made. The bust was modelled by Harkwood. Four examples appeared in Christie's sale which dissolved the Wedgwood and Bentley partnership in 1781. Addison was not worth a lot to himself and was sold with his contemporaries Swift and Pope for £4—4—6 the three.
Collection: The Dwight and Lucille Beeson Museum of Wedgwood, Birmingham, Alabama.

Left

A Wedgwood and Bentley variegated creamware ewer, marked Wedgwood and Bentley: Etruria on the black basalt plinth. Vases of this type, often as this similar in form to black basalt examples, are also set on black basalt or white jasper bases. They are marbled on every visible surface in shades of brown and green.

A single specimen of this ware today commands £350, $840 or more.

Collection: The Dwight and Lucille Beeson Museum of Wedgwood, Birmingham, Alabama.

A Wedgwood and Bentley black basalt bulb pot, mark Wedgwood and Bentley impressed. The dominant decorative motifs are the same as on the previous vase. The two rows of petal shaped nozzles are removable to allow the bulbs to be inserted.

Collection: The Dwight and Lucille Beeson Museum of Wedgwood, Birmingham, Alabama.

in heavy splashed glazes. These disguised the comparative coarseness of the creamware, which was, at its best, of a yellow colour. One of Josiah's greatest achievements was to refine this into an extremely white ware which is the direct ancestor of modern earthenware. Not only did Josiah produce creamware of a higher quality than anyone before, but he succeeded in producing it in very large quantities. This ware, which he styled 'Queensware' in honour of Queen Charlotte, his patroness, spelled the death of the tin-glazed delftwares. It was much lighter, whiter and more like porcelain. Josiah was a propagandist of the first order and managed to sell large quantities of his creamware on the Continent. Among the clients he obtained was Catherine the Great of Russia, for whom Wedgwood produced a large service painted with named views in England. Apart from this service, and one or two family armorial services which are extremely handsome, the majority of Wedgwood's creamware was decorated in an arid neo-classical style which does not recommend it to collectors. However, it was the source of the capital that financed Josiah Wedgwood's other equally successful inventions.

In 1762, at Liverpool, where many of his wares were transfer printed by Sadler and Green, Wedgwood met Thomas Bentley. Together they established a partnership and in 1768 started to build a factory at Etruria. Bentley was an enthusiastic antiquarian, whence the name *Etruria*. The first day's production of vases at the factory all bore the inscription *Artes Etruriae Renascuntur*. The shapes of the pieces produced were definitely classical in inspiration. Of these the majority were vases, library busts and pieces of a decorative nature. Josiah still produced his creamwares independently of the partnership. More important than the form of the vases and other pieces, though, was the substance from which they were made. Quite a number were produced in solid agate and variegated creamware, traditional Staffordshire materials.

45

But the most magnificent specimens were made of a new substance which in his catalogue of 1773 he described as: ' a fine black porcelain, having nearly the same properties as the basaltes, resisting the attacks of acid, being a touchstone to copper, silver and gold and equal in hardness to agate or porphyry '. This was not an entirely new material, as a black body had been used since time immemorial for tiles and was standard in Mediaeval and Roman practice. The Elers were the first to attempt to improve it. Josiah's product was composed of native clay, ironstone, ochre and manganese. The result is a very hard substance which can be polished on the lathe or decorated with engine turned patterns. Many of the black basalt vases of the Wedgwood and Bentley period have a smooth, almost lustrous surface. Many others have engine turned fluting or other such decoration. At first they were produced with plain surfaces, but Wedgwood soon went over to decorating them in low relief with foliage and classical subjects.

After vases, the finest productions in black basalt were the library busts of philosophers and writers. Apart from a thriving market in England, these sold well in Germany and Russia, whilst Holland showed a great demand for figures of Dutch interest. The majority of the finer black basalt and variegated vases, together with the black basalt busts, have the distinctive mark ' Wedgwood & Bentley, Etruria ' within a circular medallion. This must be the first example of so specific a mark in regular use. The pieces of lesser size or importance bear either the words ' Wedgwood & Bentley ' impressed, or, on very small pieces such as intaglios, the letters W & B.

The use of black basalt for intaglios, another of its earliest applications, was due to the high polish which could be achieved. In 1773–1774 these objects were produced in large numbers, often as direct copies of classical gems. They were also made with customers' initials or with portraits. A later and very subtle refinement involved intaglios made from black basalt and blue jasper, with polished bevelled edges which effectively counterfeited the two coloured classical gem. The black basalt intaglio, however, is completely overshadowed in importance by the bas-reliefs, medallions and portrait plaques which Wedgwood and Bentley produced. Those made in basalt were pressed in a mould and then finished with a modelling tool. At first they were on a small scale and comparatively unambitious, but with increasing experience Wedgwood was gradually emboldened to attempt larger and more elaborate subjects. As Wedgwood wrote to Bentley in 1774, ' Tablet making is the nicest branch of our business and requires a longer series of my attention '. He certainly gave it a large measure of attention and produced a vast and extended variety of medallions. This field was given even greater scope with the development of jasper in 1768. The themes of Wedgwood's medallions were markedly classical. This is not surprising in view of the great interest that Bentley had in the Roman era and the contemporary vogue for classical gems, vases and sculpture. The designs were executed for Wedgwood by Hackwood, Flaxman and others. At times, as with the library busts, they made improved versions of classical portrait busts. Alternatively they copied famous gems from famous cabinets such as that of Sir William Hamilton, the husband of Nelson's Emma. Some of the larger reliefs, such as ' The Death of a Roman Warrior ' are adaptations of famous Roman reliefs; others, such as ' The Battle between Jupiter and the Titans ' and ' The Feast of the Gods ' were original works in the classical vocabulary.

The number of different subjects covered by Wedgwood medallions is quite remarkable. His catalogues provide a surprising introduction to the vastness of their scope. There are some 400 different bas-reliefs, over 400 intaglios, and over 600 portrait medallions listed in the various catalogues, and several subjects produced were never listed in any of the issued catalogues. The portrait medallions fall into two groups; the Antique and the Modern. The greatest number of the former are to be found in black basalt, and were produced in sets, The Twelve Caesars, The Popes, The Kings of England and The Kings of France. The moderns, embracing Princes, Naturalists, Architects, English Poets, Philosophers, Statesmen, Physicians, Painters, Divines and other categories, were originally produced in biscuit, but the majority are to be found in blue and white jasper. The white relief applied to the blue ground offered great technical advantages over the basalt medallions. It enabled a far higher relief to be achieved in all the medallions, such as

A Wedgwood and Bentley black basalt vase and cover, mark Wedgwood and Bentley impressed. The cupids with garlands are modelled by Harkwood. This vase shows a pleasant combination of moulded relief and engine-turned flutes produced on a lathe. In 1966 this sold for £672, $1,820.

Collection: The Dwight and Lucille Beeson Museum of Wedgwood, Birmingham, Alabama.

46

A Wedgwood and Bentley black basalt ewer, marked Wedgwood and Bentley Etruria around the screw at the base: This almost certainly formed part of a *garniture* including two-handled vases and other ewers.
Collection: *The Dwight and Lucille Beeson Museum of Wedgwood, Birmingham, Alabama.*

occurs in the example illustrated, and the transparency of the white in the thinner areas gives an extra subtlety to the plaques. Many of the smaller cameos and medallions were not intended to stand by themselves, any more than were, in fact, the large plaques. Thousands of them were mounted in belt buckles, opera glasses, boxes, chatelaines, rings, lockets, buttons and other objects. Often the mounts were of cut steel produced by Matthew Boulton and James Watt at Wolverhampton. The larger plaques found their way into mantelpieces, furniture, candlesticks and other decorative interior features of the Age of Adam.

The 'jasper' mentioned several times above was evolved by Wedgwood around 1776 and produced towards the end of the 70's. In the combination of white on blue it is what many people think of today as 'Wedgwood'. In this form it is also the most frequently copied of all his products. Not merely was it blatantly imitated by several of his rivals in Staffordshire, but it was also copied at Sèvres and echoes of it are to be found in Meissen porcelain towards the end of the century. Jasper is, in Josiah's own words 'a white porcelain bisque of exquisite beauty and delicacy, possessing the general qualities of the 'Basaltes' together with that of receiving colours through its whole substance, in a manner which no other body, ancient or modern, has been known to do'. In its white state it closely resembles an unglazed porcelain. When thin it is translucent. It is extremely simple to stain it evenly and thoroughly. The result of this colouring process is known as 'solid' blue or green jasper. Alternatively the surface can be coloured with a solution of jasper which is known as a dip. This produces the finest results but is found only on certain wares of the earliest period. The colours in which jasper is made are the common blue, sage green, lilac and yellow. Though these generally occur alone, pieces also exist with three, four, or very rarely five colours together. In the early wares the edges of medallions and the interiors of cups were frequently lapidary-polished on the lathe. The dipped pieces lent themselves particularly to engine turning, with fluting and chequer patterns cut into the coloured ground to reveal the underlying white body.

The vast production of medallions and plaques apart, jasper wares are not found with the Wedgwood and Bentley mark. This is largely due to two factors: firstly, the partnership set out to produce decorative wares only—typically vases and medallions, and secondly, Bentley's death in 1780 followed fairly swiftly after the perfection of the body. The period 1780–1795 was the golden age of jasper production. During this period Josiah, untrammelled by a

A pair of Wedgwood and Bentley black basalt busts of Voltaire and Rousseau on blue and white jasper bases: the busts impressed Wedgwood and Bentley, the bases marked Wedgwood. This is a rare combination, and evidently the busts are a few years older than the bases.

Small pieces of Wedgwood and Bentley are always in demand: these busts fetched £262, $735 in 1965.

Centre

A Wedgwood blue and white pastille burner formed as a Roman altar, impressed Wedgwood, *circa* 1785. A rare shape, the ground of solid blue jasper, the white reliefs showing good translucency.

48

A Wedgwood and Bentley blue and white jasper portrait medallion of Linnaeus, impressed Wedgwood and Bentley. Linnaeus first appeared in Wedgwood's catalogue in 1778. The dark blue ground is typical of Wedgwood and Bentley period medallions. So too is the fine undercutting which makes the profile so translucent. Medallions of this date have very rectangular edges and there are almost invariably holes in the back to allow for shrinkage in the firing.

Since Linnaeus is of interest to doctors and scientists as well as to collectors, medallions such as this fetch £200, $480 today.

A Wedgwood and Bentley portrait medallion of Henry IV of France impressed Wedgwood and Bentley. Wedgwood produced medallions of the Roman Emperors, the Popes, the Kings of England and France. Many of the portraits were modelled for him by Flaxman. The title impressed on the front beneath the portrait is typical of early medallions.

£40, $104 (1965).

A blue and white jasper portrait medallion of Sir William Hamilton, marked Wedgwood. Sir William was closely connected with Josiah and many specimens from his cabinet of gems were copied in jasper and black basalt. The portrait, by Joachim Smith, is a very good example of lively modelling and characterisation which typifies the best Wedgwood portraits.

partner, and in the full flush of success, produced an ever increasing variety of wares. Teapots, cups and saucers, jugs, bowls and vases in variety, inkwells, bulb pots, and countless other items were produced. Despite the volume of production the quality of the pieces is always very high, and endorse Wedgwood's claim to be, if nothing else, the most professional potter of his age.

It was in jasper that Josiah produced the piece which set the seal on his whole range of production, the Portland vase. This, started in 1786 and finished in 1790, was a copy of the famous Roman glass vase of the 1st century B.C. now in the British Museum. Formerly in the Barberini Palace at Rome, this had been brought to England in the 1760's and subsequently passed into the Portland collection. Copies were made of it in plaster by the modeller Tassie, who was responsible for many of Wedgwood's portrait medallions. But these had a very poor surface and were not very durable. Josiah now

Wedgwood and Bentley medallion of Andromache mourning the ashes of Hector, impressed Wedgwood and Bentley. Though not a very beautiful subject, this shows the very high relief which is to be found on even the smaller medallions of the early years.

£110, $308 (1965).

Wedgwood and Bentley medallion of the Three Graces in contemporary ormolu frame by Boulton and Watt. Modelled by Flaxman, this small medallion is a particularly fine example with translucent white relief.

£160, $450 (1965).

had in his jasper a material of great durability. The white overlay had proved to be capable of reproducing the effect of the Roman glass. It had the subtlety and translucency which hitherto was only to be found in glass. The greatest problem was of course, the ground. The colour of the ordinary blue jasper, which is definitely pale, is far different from that of the dark greenish blue, turned almost black by time, of the glass original. Josiah experimented extensively with this. The final result, to be seen in the limited edition of fifty produced, was an excellent demonstration of his technical mastery over materials. Although it is officially solid dark blue jasper, the ground colour is hardly distinguishable from plain black. Only in very rare examples, such as the one illustrated, is the colour genuinely blue. These few were probably experimental vases produced before the definitive edition itself. Only three or four of these Portland vases, known as 'slate blue', survive. Of the orthodox edition, of which most of the vases are numbered, some sixteen to

Two Wedgwood blue and white jasper scent flaçons, *circa* 1785. Perhaps the only pieces which, owing to their shape, had no place for the Wedgwood mark to be impressed. Examples are to be found with gold and enamel mounts.

A Wedgwood blue and white jasper buckle with contemporary shagreen and cut steel mounts by Boulton and Watt. *Circa* 1785. The two plaques of Poor Maria and the Shepherd Boy are not uncommon in themselves but buckles of this sort are rare and coveted by collectors of Wedgwood and their wives.

twenty remain. On these the white jasper reliefs tend to have a yellowish tone, perhaps caused by the blackish grounds. The slate blue examples, on the other hand, have kept the whiteness of their reliefs. Josiah launched his Portland vases with very skilful propaganda. This invested them with an immense cachet which has endured to this day. No Wedgwood collection is really complete without a Portland vase, but of the few now remaining many are already in permanent collections.

The death of Josiah Wedgwood in 1795 really saw the end of the great era of production at the factory. Throughout the 19th century the creamwares, basalts and jasper continued to be made. Often they were mere reproductions of the earlier wares. The quality fell off considerably and the attention to the finishing of pieces was much less. The great Exhibition did engender a special edition of plaques, often in three colours, of a rather finer quality, but still not as lovingly made as the wares of the first period. But the century produced three significant developments. For a few years, between 1812 and 1816, a fine bone china was made, marked with the word Wedgwood in red. These, decorated in the simple neo-classical style prevalent at the time, seriously impinged on the creamware market and the ware was therefore discontinued. As a result it is extremely rare. In about 1822 the second innovation, known as 'Moonlight Lustre', was introduced. This was a pink lustre such as was generally made in Staffordshire and Sunderland at the period. The fineness of the potting and the standard of the decoration are higher than most contemporary products from other factories. Like the bone china these pieces are very hard to find. The 1860's saw the third new phenomenon. This was the elaborate decoration of creamware dishes, plaques and vases by Emile Lessore. These were painted in a figurative style with scenes after Rubens and other artists or with pastoral subjects.

Of all English porcelains made in the present century, Wedgwood 'Fairyland Lustre', produced in 1917 from designs by Daisy Makeig-Jones, are unusually sought after. These were decorated in dark flambé lustre colours and gilt from engraved copper plates, with designs of which the illustrated bowl is typical. The reason for the competition which these wares inspire is that they were in production for a very short time only before the expense of making them became prohibitive. The scarcity of the ware combines with a considerable demand from American collectors to make Fairyland Lustre increasingly expensive.

The interest in Wedgwood throughout the United States, which exceeds by far that devoted by collectors to any other single factory, has had a radical effect on the prices of all the factory's products, almost regardless of age. However, the great enthusiasm which it engenders in America today is really no greater than that shown by collectors in the last century. In fact from the very start Wedgwood himself produced his basalt and jasper for a collectors' market. It was successful right from the beginning and those who then and later have bought Wedgwood have found it a good investment. By an extraordinary chance the price for Wedgwood from the earliest moments is fully documented. Not merely do we know the prices at which they were

A pair of Wedgwood blue and white jasper square jardinières, impressed Wedgwood *Circa* 1785. The sides have cupids emblematic of the Four Seasons.
Centre
A Wedgwood blue and white jasper milk jug, impressed Wedgwood in lower case. 1778-80.

held in the warehouse of Wedgwood & Bentley in Chelsea; we also know many of the reduced prices set by Josiah after Bentley's death. Also we have the vital information contained in Christie & Ansell's sale of March 1781 in which all the wares belonging to the partnership were dispersed at auction in Pall Mall. As the frontispiece of the catalogue states, the sale contained a wide variety of wares embracing all the aspects of the partnership's production.

The 19th century saw a series of sales of Wedgwood at auction, some of which lasted for several days. These show what pieces in particular were in demand in the Victorian era. Recent years too have witnessed some interesting sales, not all of them large, but on several occasions pieces have appeared in the Rooms which have passed under the hammer before. Others too have passed through which can be compared with previous similar examples. In the last ten years, for instance, collectors had the rare opportunity on three occasions of competing for Portland vases of the first edition, two of them black and the other one of the very few slate blue examples. The first of these black examples was sold at Sotheby in 1956, and fetched £480, $1,150. It was not till July 1963 that the next one came up for sale, this time at Christie's. This particular example had a very interesting history. It was purchased by the then Duke of Marlborough from Wedgwood for 33 guineas. Just under a century later it came up for auction at Christie's, for the first time in 1886 and fetched 155 guineas. On its second appearance at auction it was purchased by a Chicago collector for 1,350 guineas, $3,400. Just over a year later the slate blue copy came up for sale. This too made two appearances at auction. In 1902 it was sold by the executors of J. L. Propert, a noted collector of Wedgwood, and was bought for Mrs Spranger. It is not known how much Propert paid for the vase, or even precisely how he acquired it. In his sale it fetched 380 guineas. In the 60 years that then elapsed this important and unusual piece, though it was illustrated in almost every 19th century work on Wedgwood and had been frequently exhibited whilst Propert had it, sank into oblivion. It remained all the time safely in the Spranger family till sold by them in 1964 for 2,900 guineas, $7,300. It, too, is now in America.

A triple spill vase formed as ruined truncated columns, impressed Wedgwood. Pieces of this type with a deliberately battered appearance are among Wedgwood's ingenious conceits and very much in the spirit of the age. They are extremely hard to find today.

Collection: The Dwight and Lucille Beeson Museum of Wedgwood, Birmingham, Alabama.

The fact that a vase sold in 1902 for 380 guineas sold in 1964 for 2,900 guineas is no more remarkable in a way than the price realised by the first perfect Portland vase ever sold at auction. In 1856 the poet Samuel Rogers died. His executors' sale, which consisted in the main of Attic and Etruscan vases, also included a first edition Portland vase, then about 60 years old. This, which he had bought for less than £50 when new, now sold for 127 guineas. Another similar vase, from a less distinguished source brought only 97 guineas in the same year. Of the five other Portland vases which were sold at auction during the last century, two only were sold for higher prices. Of these, the first was the Marlborough vase, whilst the second belonged to Cornelius Cox, whose sale, containing 721 lots, lasted for four days and realised a total of £6,242. Of this, the Portland vase contributed 200 guineas.

The Portland vase, though Wedgwood's most famous creation, does not provide us with a true yardstick of the way Wedgwood has changed in value over the years. The original copies were very much more expensive than other pieces of Wedgwood, or the other English porcelains produced at the same date. They also attract a very limited field of collectors. A word of caution at this stage. No Portland vase of the original edition bears any identifying mark to suggest that it is Wedgwood, save for a pencilled number to be found on the inside of the neck. Examples are to be found with the impressed Wedgwood mark. These all date from the 19th century and are generally of much lower quality. One may easily be acquired for £40 or £50, $100–$120. The greatest appreciation is to be found among the wares of the Wedgwood & Bentley period. There is perhaps no other mark which has so radical an effect on the value of the pieces on which it appears. The original marbled vases were sold by Wedgwood & Bentley in sets of five, three or seven. Unfortunately the 18th century lists do not generally specify the height of the pieces. Sets of vases sold for between 10s. and 15s. for each vase in the set. During the last century the price rose to a certain extent so that in the sale of the Barlow collection at Christie's, May 4th, 1869, a 'pair of crystalline agate vases, classical form, with gilt handles and garlands, reversible for candlesticks, 10 ins. high, marked Wedgwood and Bentley', what today we

A Wedgwood slate blue Portland Vase, 10 in. high. This is probably a precursor of the black and white examples produced by Josiah Wedgwood in the closing years of his life. The white relief is particularly finely cut and shows a very skilful use of the translucency of the material which came very close to imitating the reliefs on the Roman glass original. Like all the first edition Portland Vases this is unmarked. Vases marked Wedgwood are invariably of later date and generally of poor quality. Often the base, which in the early examples has a head in a Phrygian cap, is not even decorated. This vase sold for 380 guineas in 1902. In 1964 it fetched 2,900 guineas, $8,525. An example of the black ground type made 1,350 guineas, $3,976 in 1963. A 19th century example would fetch perhaps £100, $240.

A selection of teawares in blue and white jasper: all are of finely potted and finished jasper which is much more delicate than the pieces made today.

52

A three coloured dice pattern bulb pot and liner, impressed Wedgwood. *Circa* 1785. The white ground is dipped in blue and decorated with chequer pattern on the lathe. The applied rosettes are sage green. This type of ware continued into the 19th century, but the early pieces, which are very translucent and thinly potted are very fine: a single coffee cup and saucer might cost £150, $360.

A lilac jasper teapot and cover, impressed Wedgwood. *Circa* 1785. This is dipped in lilac and has engine turned flutes and applied classical reliefs. Probably the rarest colour of jasper, pieces in lilac are usually of good quality and justifiably expensive.

A Wedgwood creamware ewer painted by Emile Lessore *circa* 1880. The decoration is untypical of Lessore's normal style which is rather soft and insipid.
This ewer with its companion fetched £400, $1,120 in 1966 and is now in an American collection

A Chelsea group of the Dutch or Tyrolean Dancers: red anchor period. This model was conceived at Meissen by J. J. Kändler, but is to be found at Bow, Derby, here at Chelsea and in Chinese export porcelain. Of all the versions the Chelsea one is probably the most highly valued.

would call 'cassolettes', sold for £11. In the same sale a 'porphyry vase, with winged figures, handles gilt and ribbon garlands, 9 ins. high' made £4. 10s. Today vases of this type have increased a hundred fold and it would be extremely difficult to acquire a perfect example for much less than £400, $1,000.

Black basalt is dearer still, though its original price was about the same as the variegated wares. In 1869 a black basalt vase, after a model by Flaxman, 16 ins. high, sold for £7. A vase answering to the same description turned up in 1966 and sold for £672, $1,610. Black basalt in general, even when not of the earliest period, is the object of great competition and therefore liable to go on appreciating. So too are all medallions bearing the Wedgwood & Bentley mark. The portraits were sold by Josiah for between three shillings and ten and sixpence. Today portraits of the first period realise three figure sums, depending to a certain extent on the quality of the modelling. Even portrait plaques bearing only the mark 'Wedgwood', if of good quality, fetch fairly high prices. Large basalt plaques such as the 'Feast of the Gods' which in the Wedgwood & Bentley sale sold for £1. 2s. for a set of five would be worth today several hundred pounds each. A century ago the large reliefs, generally in jasper, which were large and showy pieces that appealed to the Victorian appetite, achieved tremendously high prices. Higher in fact than they might today. So too did large jasper vases. In the sale of the Sibson Collection in 1877, an event which lasted two days and realised £7,473, Lot 286, 'A magnificent vase, black jasper, with serpent handles and heads of Medusa, bands of Grecian ornament in white: subject the Apotheosis of Homer, the cover surmounted by Pegasus on large square pedestal with griffins at the angles and figures at each side', realised 750 guineas. This remained until 1963 the highest price paid at auction for a single piece of Wedgwood. It is unlikely, if vases of this type, generally called Pegasus vases, came up for sale today, that they would fetch anything like this price, any more than massive Chelsea vases of the gold anchor period. Fortunately, the majority of these massive *tours-de-force* are already in museums, such as the Metropolitan Museum of Art. Collectors of Wedgwood today tend to concentrate on the smaller pieces: medallions, scent bottles and jewellery. Alternatively the unusual pieces are sought after: three colour jasper wares, cosmetic and paint boxes, custard cups, chessmen, even pestles and mortars. Wedgwood & Bentley's sole useful products are collected for their rarity as much as any other qualities they may also have. Every collection should contain representative pieces of the black basalt and jasper wares; but the individual nature of one collection is based on those pieces which are unlikely to be found in others. In Wedgwood, as in anything else, these are the most likely to appreciate.

No collection of Wedgwood wares is really complete without pieces made by his foremost imitators. Both blue and white jasper and black basalt were copied on a fairly large scale around the end of the 18th century. Adams of

Tunstall, Turner of Lane End, Mayer of Hanley, the Hollins family and Leeds all made wares in the Wedgwood style. The jaspers of Adams, Turner and Hollins can be extremely fine. Mayer of Hanley specialised in black basalt wares with particularly attractive engine turned decoration. Leeds made medallions of classical portraits reminiscent of those by Wedgwood & Bentley, but lacking in the finished characteristic of all the products of Josiah Wedgwood. Hollins's pieces are rare, and his jaspers are extremely fine. So too are those of Adams and Turner. The solid blue grounds are of a shade different from the Wedgwood blue jasper, but the subjects are often precisely the same. Turner, like Wedgwood, had his eye fixed strongly on the continental market. To this end he produced a fine creamware. This he shipped to Holland and decorated there in his own enamelling shop. He also decorated Leeds and Wedgwood creamwares. The subjects that occur on these pieces are broadly of three types. Numerous pieces occur with portraits of the Prince and Princess of Orange. Others depict religious themes. The seven sacraments, subjects from the Old Testament, Crucifixion scenes and Our Lady of Kevelaar, a local pilgrimage centre. All these wares are very colourful and carefully, if somewhat gauchely, decorated. In view of their immense and unsophisticated decorative qualities, they are not at all expensive at present and are liable to rise in value in the future.

The wares of followers and imitators of Josiah Wedgwood have not as yet received the almost passionate adulation that early Wedgwood products have enjoyed in the United States. Today, however, when Wedgwood competes with the major early porcelain factories in price, it is very difficult to embark on a collection of Wedgwood wares without a fair amount of capital to play with. The other factories have recently gained esteem as a result of research which has shown more clearly the scope of their production and their individual originality. So they, too, have begun to increase faster in value.

A Fairyland Lustre punchbowl, *circa* 1918. This shows a typical example of the many coloured decoration with lustrous surface and gilt outline.
In 1967 this bowl was sold for £150, $420.

Eleven various jasper plaques of the first period: the bevelled edges, which are polished on the wheel, are generally a sign of 18th century origin. The three horizontal plaques are in three colour jasper in either blue, green and white or pink, green and white. The larger upright oval is a particularly good example of the white relief which is translucent and of a dipped ground which produces the white bevelled border.

All these pieces are marked WEDGWOOD.

LEEDS

The refinement of creamware was not exploited by Wedgwood alone. At Leeds a pottery was established in the late 1750's and its success and long life were second only to that of Josiah's factory. The creamware of Leeds is physically the same as that of Wedgwood, but the appearance and form of the wares are different. Wedgwood potted his teapots, plates, and dishes without foot rims. His early wares were markedly yellow in colour, his later productions a creamy white. Those of Leeds began by being a little less yellow in tinge but never achieved the even whiteness of Wedgwood Queensware.

The shapes assumed by teapots, coffee pots, jugs and other wares are much the same at both factories. However, it is in the handles and finials that Leeds is particularly distinctive. The handles, which are often reeded, or formed as two interlaced loops, were attached to the main body of the piece by rosettes. Many of these rosettes have leaves to either side. These terminals were frequently enriched in the same colours as the rest of the piece. The finials are usually formed as flower sprays.

The wares of the Leeds factory fall into different groups. The basic sort are the undecorated pieces, generally dating from the opening years of the factory's production. At their plainest these are simple pieces, the only focus of interest being the handles which were discussed above. At their most complex they include épergnes, cocklepots, cruet stands, chestnut baskets, sweetmeat stands, melon-shaped tureens and other fanciful pieces. These were all illustrated in the company's Pattern Book, issued in several languages and definitely beamed at the Continental market, just as were Wedgwood's handouts. The principal beauty of these pieces is often the perforated patterns which were one of the factory's individual contributions. This decorative device may well have had an economic as well as an aesthetic reason behind it. Imports to certain parts of the Continent were charged duty according to their weight; the perforations in most cases enabled the potters to produce lighter, but equally useful pieces.

Many pieces of Leeds creamware, like many of Wedgwood's manufacture, were sent to Liverpool in the white. There they were decorated with transfer-

A Leeds perforated white melon tureen and stand: competing with the more sophisticated porcelain manufacturers the Leeds factory also produced elaborate pieces such as this. The piercing of the cover is typical of the perforations to be found on plates, cockle pots and other pieces.

A Leeds toast rack. This illustrates the virtuosity of the Leeds factory which showed in its pattern book a prodigious variety of useful and ornamental wares.

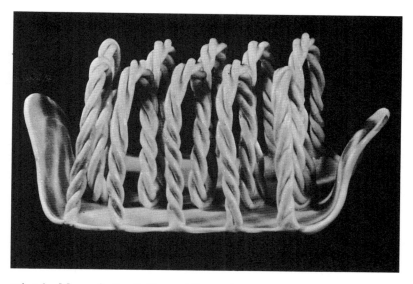

prints by Messrs. Sadler & Green. These prints are often very similar to those found on Worcester porcelain, including as they do a plagiarised version of the Tea Party and a variety of pastoral scenes similar to those to be seen at Worcester. Several pieces definitely made at Leeds and Etruria appear with the same prints. Services were quite possibly made up indiscriminately from the wares of Leeds and Wedgwood. Just as Worcester produced armorial wares in the manner of Oriental Lowestoft, the Leeds factory decorated creamware with coats-of-arms for their clients. Pieces of this type are fairly uncommon. Particularly fine and interesting is the whole range of wares produced in the Whieldon style and splashed with tortoiseshell and other glazes. Some of the rarer teapots even have three mask feet in the earlier fashion, but the majority of the pieces are inspired by, rather than imitate, the agate wares of the preceding generation. Some of the marbled pieces are extremely original and attractive. The bowl illustrated is a very good example of this ware at its best.

At the Leeds factory large numbers of the wares were decorated with simple floral decoration, while other pieces were painted by the enameller David Rhodes who also worked on Wedgwood wares. Typical of his work are vertical striped patterns, ladies with birds in red and black and floral motifs in a similar palette. Another part of the factory's production was sent undecorated to Holland where it was enamelled at Turner's workshop. The majority of the pieces that were so treated were flatwares. More unusual and therefore more interesting are the shaped pieces that occur. Of these the most extraordinary is a spittoon. Among the other shapes are tea caddies, sugar basins and other teawares.

All the earlier Leeds wares are unmarked. It was not until fairly late in the century that the words ' Leeds Pottery ' were impressed on the factory's products. This development was more or less simultaneous with the introduction of pearl ware. This was a creamware covered in an off-white glaze with a slightly blue cast. The wares produced in this are fairly uninspired. When not transfer-printed in blue with designs of the usual type prevalent everywhere they tend to display pseudo-*famille rose* patterns not unsimilar to those found on contemporary New Hall wares. Another change that accompanied the arrival of creamware was the increase in the production of figures. These were never made in large numbers, but included figures of musicians which were generally undecorated and figures of stallions which must be among the largest and most massive examples of English pottery. These appear decorated in a variety of techniques, many examples with sponged decoration of a Pratt type. Till recently these were regarded as very rare, but recent publicity following the high prices realised by two examples in 1967 has brought many hitherto unregarded specimens on to the market. It will be interesting to see which way the trend develops in this particular instance. The production of these horses continued till at least 1840 and they must be

among the latest productions to be seriously collected, excluding of course the Portrait Figures of the Victorian era.

Apart from the few figures that are to be found, pearl wares are not much in demand today. They lack the quality or originality necessary to arouse interest. Only the unusual Batavian wares with their rather extraordinary decoration are liable to appreciate, owing to their rarity and strangeness. Dutch decorated wares, which should really embrace all the different cream-wares enamelled at Turner's workshop, can be extremely fine, and are still not expensive compared with other types. Of course, here again, the quality and originality of the piece must be carefully considered. Many pieces can be found with portraits of the Stadholder William V of Orange Nassau and

62

Left

A Leeds figure of a Stallion. These large figures were sold to Saddlers, Farriers and other tradesmen connected with the world of horses. They were made in creamware and pearlware and their decoration varies quite widely, some having a very Prattlike appearance. Until fairly recently these were not highly valued. This one sold for £1,050, $2,940, in May 1967. Since then there have been several on the market which have fetched between £800 and £1,750, $1,900 and $4,200. This is a sphere where a great uncertainty prevails since there are many more of these than originally appeared likely.

Right

A Leeds marbled bowl: this should be compared with Wedgwood's variegated creamwares. Of course, since it is not Wedgwood a bowl of this type is in comparison, not expensive (£50, $120).

A Leeds granite jug, the surface speckled in grey, the border with chequer pattern in black.

his consort, but only a few rise above the ordinary run. Some of them are to be found in numbered sets, each with different expressions of loyalty on the borders. Many of the single specimens to be seen once formed part of such series, which are much more valuable when complete. This explains the odd numbers which are to be found on pieces. Sets of the Sacraments can be extremely fine, though these, and the many pieces depicting the Crucifixion and other Biblical events tend to suffer from an unwillingness among many people to buy pieces with religious associations. Rare forms, as mentioned above, and subjects out of the normal run are the best to acquire, though as always, these are not easily found.

The transfer-printed wares illustrate the way in which, ultimately, no

A Leeds Batavian ware tea caddy. The decoration of this is inspired by Oriental porcelains with blue and white panels on *café-au-lait* grounds. This is a pearlware rather than a creamware, but the form of the teacaddy is to be found in Leeds of all periods.

Three Leeds creamware armorial plates: the arms are those of: *left*, unidentified.
Right Richard Hely Hutchinson, 1st Earl of Donoughmore.
Below right Richard Grenville, Marquess of Buckingham.

English factory goes unaffected by interest in the others. The Leeds wares decorated at Liverpool by Sadler & Green are closely related to Wedgwood and other wares similarly treated; but they also have much in common, not merely with the porcelains, such as Bow and Worcester, but with opaque glass and enamels which were all used as vehicles for transfer printed decoration. As a result, they appeal to a different type of collector, one who collects different types of print rather than different shapes or pastes. Since transfer-printed decoration in its earliest years was limited to single colours its decorative qualities are somewhat restricted. The collector of printed pieces is a true lover of ceramics, because the interest of these is not an obvious external one, but an intrinsic and subtle quality only appreciated by those who really have a deep feeling for the material. This is also a phase of development in English ceramic manufacture which was closely bound up with the Industrial Revolution and fundamental to subsequent developments. Until lately these pieces, in all their forms, were not sufficiently regarded, but recent research has concentrated a great deal of energy on the field of transfer-printed decoration and its development. As a result the collector of all transfer-printed wares is in a much better-informed position than he would have been only a few years ago. Nothing breeds confidence in the Art Market like knowledge. The purchaser of a transfer-printed piece can find out a lot about it, thus increasing his enjoyment of his possession. The dull undecorative colouring will, however, have one effect on this group of wares. It will always prevent transfer-printed wares from realizing any but evenly increasing prices and will deprive this particular side of the market of any unexpected jumps in value.

This steady, though undramatic, rise in prices must basically apply also to the early white wares from Leeds, whether plain or decorated with perforations. White wares never fetch the same sort of prices that otherwise similar but coloured examples attract. At the same time these creamwares were the first to be sufficiently refined to permit their use undecorated. They are examples of good but simple taste in potting which combine all the charm of craftsmanship with the first appearance of 'modern' earthenwares. It should be noted that white creamwares of great complexity are to be found, often bearing impressed 'Leeds Pottery' marks: these are not old and should be given a wide berth.

For one pottery Leeds offers a very wide variety of interest, with forms and types of decoration for all tastes. While there is now a steady interest in its products there is little likelihood of a staggering reappraisal in its value. It would be a mistake to form a collection of anything, and especially porcelain and pottery, using potential appreciation as the sole criterion. A far more reliable policy is to concentrate on quality and rarity. For while collectors may wish in the future to know whether a piece has been expensive in the past, and may assess current worth on the basis of its previous price, in the last analysis the intrinsic merit and appeal of the object will play the major part in determining its value.

STAFFORDSHIRE FIGURES

The most recent newcomer to the collectors' shelves and the international market is the great group of Staffordshire Pottery Figures which were produced throughout Queen Victoria's reign and even overflowed slightly into this century. Just as the delft wares often represent a popular commentary on contemporary events in the late 17th and early 18th centuries, and Ralph Wood and the potters at Leeds and throughout Staffordshire recorded national and local events, so in an industrialised age the potter produced figures that recorded the most prominent characters and events of the day. Compared with the carefully potted and extremely individual creations of the 18th century, however, the Victorian Staffordshire figures are crude. They were mostly made in two pieces in moulds and a great proportion of the decoration was farmed out to outside decorators. As a result there is a great variation in the quality of different examples of the same figure.

The most significant group of figures, a type which persists through the whole of Queen Victoria's reign, is formed by figures and groups of the Queen and her ever increasing family. The Queen herself and the Prince Consort appear in many different guises and attitudes: on horseback, with the young Princess Royal, enthroned in robes of State. Some of the figures are named on the base, others are not. Some again are clearly recognisable portraits, whilst others require considerable imagination to see in them the Queen and the Prince Consort. The childhood, education, marriage and later the accession of Edward VII in 1901 are all commemorated. So too are the marriages of his sisters to the Duke of Argyll and William II of Prussia, father of the Kaiser. Prince Arthur also appears as a companion to his brother.

Prince Albert.
The Duke of Wellington.
Lord Raglan.
The figure of the Prince Consort shows how well modelled and decorated the figures can be on rare occasions.
Raglan is among the rarer of the figures dating from the Crimean War. This is perhaps explained by his relative unpopularity. Wellington occurs more frequently in civilian dress than uniform since his life during the period in which portrait figures were produced was mainly political.

68

The British Royal family did not hold a monopoly of attention. Napoleon III and the Empress Eugénie enjoyed great popularity in England at the time of the Crimean War and inspired some of the finest figures produced in the century. The King of Sardinia and the Shah of Persia both visited London during Victoria's reign. The King appears in a distinguished group with the Queen and his favourite dalmatian, which he brought with him (the advantage of a quarantine-free age). The Shah did not come off so well. The group commemorating his visit appeared only in white examples, most of which have tended by now to yellow and are of very poor quality. The Crimean war, apart from Napoleon and Eugénie, provided the inspiration for a whole series of figures and groups. The best of these are of the prominent personalities in the Allied cause: Lord Raglan, Canrobert, Marshal St. Arnaud, Havelock, Florence Nightingale and others, many of them very fine models. As well as these, there are numerous emblematic groups of a patriotic or sentimental type, some of which can be found in well modelled and finely coloured examples. Throughout the Victorian era smaller wars, the Italian War of Independence, the Franco-Prussian war, the River War, the Indian Mutiny and the Boer War also provided inspiration to the potters of portrait figures. Garibaldi appears in various attitudes, including very fine groups where he is shown standing beside his horse. He is sometimes paired with his English friend, Colonel Peard. (The parochial British outlook on life influences even our potters.) The Indian Mutiny features Highland Jessie listening to the distant pipes of the relieving army. The Franco-Prussian war produced only a series of equestrian figures of French and German generals, often from the same mould with different names on the base. The River War gave rise to many figures of General Gordon, invariably dressed in an orange tunic, whilst the Boer War, which saw out Queen Victoria, and to all intents and purposes Staffordshire portrait figures, caused a rash of extremely dull equestrian figures of generals.

War was not the only form of violence that attracted comment from the potter during this period. The British public has always followed murder cases with lurid interest and even the staid morality of the Victorian age failed to suppress this. Thus James Rush, who was hanged at Norwich for the murder of his landlord, Mr Jerney, inspired no less than five different subjects: himself, his mistress, and models of his house, Potash Farm, Stanfield Hall, Jerney's house, and Norwich Jail, where he was imprisoned. William Palmer, another murderer, also achieved immortality in pottery, whilst his house is one of the finest buildings which occurs in pottery of that period. The Irish Patriot, William Smith O'Brien, and his wife, also appear in Staffordshire pottery; O'Brien himself dramatically manacled. Another patriot from abroad was the Hungarian revolutionary Kossuth, in London in 1848.

Domestic politics, then as today, were the subject of great popular interest. This is reflected in the figures of Sir Robert Peel, Disraeli, Gladstone and his wife. It is interesting that Gladstone was either paired off with his wife or with Disraeli. Lady Beaconsfield does not appear. Sir Robert is depicted on horseback resplendent in a top hat. The Duke of Wellington, the 'Grand Old Man' of the era, had changed from a soldier into a politician before the potters portrayed him. As a result, the great warrior is shown either seated in a Gothic armchair, or standing in a frock-coat and looking every bit the smart civilian. The social conscience of the age of Elizabeth Fry and Florence Nightingale is reflected in figures of Joseph Gurney, Elizabeth Fry's brother, and Lord Shaftesbury, both unusually well-modelled figures.

The world of entertainment, the circus, the theatre and the music hall provided perhaps the most vivid subjects of all to the potters of the day. Jenny Lind, 'the Swedish Nightingale' is depicted in two different roles, as 'Alice' in *Robert le Diable* by Meyerbeer, and as 'Maria' in Donizetti's *La Figlia del Reggimento*. Her impresario Jullien also appears. So, too, do the Cushman sisters who performed a very successful *Romeo and Juliet*. From the circus comes a group variously known as 'Mr Hemming's Circus Act', or 'The Elephant of Siam', John Solomon Rarey, the American horse tamer, and many others. Many of the figures that are at present unidentified were probably inspired by contemporary actors, singers or performers and were modelled after wood engravings or lithographs from magazines such as The Illustrated London News, or music sheets which generally had coloured

pictures on the covers. Of these the majority probably represent figures whose fame was only shortlived and whose names were not impressed or gilt on the figures. This field is still full of scope for would-be researchers and figures that fall into this category have a considerable speculative value.

Contemporary actors were not the only ones to attract the potters' attention. Garrick and Kean, both as Richard III, were made, whilst Kean also appears as Hamlet. Religion too made its contribution to the subject matter of Victorian portrait figures and both contemporary and historical figures are depicted. The preachers John Wesley and Charles Spurgeon feature in various Gothic niches, while the United States is represented by the Evangelists Sankey and Moody who both made visits to England. Among other contemporary religious figures are Cardinal Manning and Pope Pius X, who appear somewhat curiously dressed. There are also to be found a wide series of groups depicting scenes from the Bible, which are usually of extremely fine quality, and, although religious subjects are today often at a discount, much sought after.

Other Americans beside Sankey and Moody were recorded by the portrait potter. Miss Amelia Bloomer was shown flaunting the garment to which she gave her name. Uncle Tom and Eva form many varied and attractive groups, mostly with different quotations from *Uncle Tom's Cabin*. Of famous contemporary politicians only Lincoln is to be found on horseback. Washington and Franklin were the objects of a certain amount of confusion in the potters' minds and many figures were produced looking like Benjamin Franklin, but unequivocally named ' Washington '. Like Harriet Beecher Stowe, Robert

Sir Robert and Lady Sale.
Jenny Lind. *page* 73
The Sales have been almost entirely lost to memory as their story was news for only a very short time in 1842. Jenny Lind, however, is of interest internationally owing to her connections with both Sweden and Australia. She has been consistently the most expensive personality.

A Liverpool blue and white potiche and cover from William Ball's factory. This apparently unique piece is probably the largest creation of the English 18th century manufacturers. For a single and unrepeated specimen from a short lived factory it displays a remarkable confidence in the decoration and shows Liverpool as a producer of major pieces.

A. J. H. du Boulay collection

Six pieces of English blue and white porcelain from various factories, showing some different characteristics.

Top right
A Derby sauceboat. The blue has a distinctly violet tinge when compared with that of the other factories.

Top left
A Liverpool oval sauceboat, possibly from Gilbody's factory; the blue on this is much clearer and the painting extremely free.

Centre
A Derby sauceboat. The violet tones in the blue again show out strongly. A small Liverpool vase—Gilbody's factory.

Below right
A Worcester mug. Painted with a typical Worcester pattern.

Below left
A bow bell-shaped mug. The blue of Bow is much flatter than that of the other factories and the decoration very stylized and dry.

John Southern Collection

Burns and William Shakespeare are represented by Tam O'Shanter and Souter Johnnie and various characters from plays. Both writers appear themselves; Burns with Highland Mary and Shakespeare generally paired with Milton, as at Derby a century before. 1854 saw Shakespeare's tercentenary, commemorated in Staffordshire by various models of his house at Stratford-upon-Avon in Warwickshire. Other authors who won the potters' attention were Byron and Sir Walter Scott. Evidently Keats, Shelley, Browning and Tennyson did not have the common touch required to gain the doubtful honour of seeing themselves rendered a thousand times in pottery.

The foregoing catalogue shows that among contemporary and historical figures there was often no particular rhyme or reason behind the process of selection. This applies to their interest to collectors and also to their value. Twenty years ago the majority of Staffordshire portrait figures could be bought for a few pounds, if not shillings. The 1950s, however, saw the formation of several collections of portrait figures and the publication of books and articles on the subject. The foremost of these were *Victorian Staffordshire Figures* by Brian Latham and *Staffordshire Portrait Figures of the Victorian Age* by Thomas Balston. Latham's book was virtually the first to explore the subject, whilst Balston's attempted the first classification of the figures and the various models in which a particular character may be found. Since it was the first classification, this has left scope for further work on the subject. In 1963 a supplement to the book was brought out and no doubt many more discoveries are still to be made. At present Balston's classification is fundamental to the would-be collectors' understanding of the subject. It is also the scaffolding around which all sale room catalogues have been constructed, for in 1963 Brian Latham's collection was the first major assembly of Staffordshire portrait figures to be offered at auction. It afforded to the public the first opportunity to see just how great was the general interest. It also gave a yardstick for the relative values of the different figures. This has since been modified by other sales of collections of figures. But from all of these various things have become clear: collecting Staffordshire figures on an extensive scale has come to stay, not merely in Britain but also in America, and to a certain extent, on the Continent of Europe. Each dispersal of a collection is eagerly greeted by newer collectors, many of whom are forming their collections with a view to eventual disposal at a profit. So far no figures of great importance from the Latham or more recent named sales have reappeared at auction. One can forecast with assurance however, an increase in value when they do. With the exception of the rarest figures, which will always be in great demand, figures from named collections seem to bring higher prices than otherwise identical ones of unknown provenance.

The most serious interest is definitely centred on figures of contemporary characters as distinct from those historical ones that caught the imagination of the potters. Of these most of the best were made between Queen Victoria's accession in 1837 and about 1850. The figures from this period are generally well coloured and quite often well modelled. Although there are good figures from later in the century, such as Sir Robert and Lady Sale and King Edward VII and Queen Alexandra, there is a great tendency in the later figures to find poor or almost no modelling and very little colouring apart from scanty gilding and painting on the faces. Of this decadence the series of equestrian figures of the Boer War generals is the epitome.

Although there has been an immense percentage increase in the value of Staffordshire figures, they are still very much more readily available to collectors than any of the pieces I have discussed in my previous chapters. A collector with a few hundred pounds or dollars to lay out could form quite a representative collection, whilst the same outlay would merely scratch the surface of Chelsea, Worcester, Ralph Wood or Delft wares. In the major 18th century fields the most rare and important pieces fetch prices into four figures. The auction record in Victorian Staffordshire is held by a group known as the ' Grapplers ', but this is the only single example to have sold for over £100, $240. Jenny Lind, Jenny Jones, William Smith O'Brien and other rare characters of fine quality all make prices over £70, $170, and from these eventually the first figure sold for £100 should emerge. It is interesting to note that the figures of Sir Robert and Lady Sale, famous for her escape from the Afghans in 1842, are by far the most eagerly pursued of later figures.

James B Rush

Emily Sandford

James Rush.
William Palmer.
Emily Sandford.
The three major criminals depicted in
Staffordshire pottery. In 1963 Rush and
Sandford fetched £50, $140 together. By
1966 the price was almost doubled and
since there has been a general shortage of
goods in this particular market since 1966
it is likely that the next examples to appear
will show further increases.

While it is difficult to foresee which way a particular market will develop,
significant trends can be noted. It is unlikely that unnamed, purely decorative
subjects will ever be seriously collected. Nor do the historical portrait figures
seem to generate the interest accorded to contemporary persons. Those
figures that seem to be making good prices today are unlikely to suffer any loss
in value in the immediate future. Even in a sphere where quality would not
appear to be a notable feature, it is ultimately the quality that will determine
the appreciation in value, or desirability of a particular piece.

74

CHELSEA

CHELSEA WARES

It is unusual for the first venture in any field to be the best. The Chelsea factory, which was, by a short head, the first to be established in England, is generally regarded as the best. Just as the greatest English silver of the day was produced by a Huguenot Frenchman, Paul de Lamerie, so it was a Huguenot, Nicholas Sprimont, himself also a silversmith, who was the driving force behind the factory's success.

The production of Sprimont's factory falls broadly into four periods. The first, known as the Triangle Period, covers the years 1745–1748. During this time Sprimont was in partnership with John Gouyn, an Englishman who had acquired some knowledge of the process used at the French soft paste factory at St. Cloud founded some years before. They obtained workmen from Staffordshire—already an important centre for pottery. During this phase Sprimont was very much a newcomer to the craft, and the dominant role in the partnership was definitely played by Gouyn. It was almost certainly he who was responsible for the famous goat-and-bee jugs, some of which bear the date 1745. However, Sprimont's training as a silversmith is shown in the crayfish salts which closely resemble contemporary examples in silver. Fundamentally, though, the products of this period are extremely scarce and are mostly to be found in museums.

The last two years of the decade saw a parting of the ways: the partnership between Sprimont and Gouyn came to an end, and the team of workmen from Staffordshire set up on their own account to form a secondary factory.

An early white teapot and cover *circa* 1746. Incised triangle mark under the base. This piece, representing a guinea fowl trapped in a rose bush, embodies all the characteristics of the incised triangle period. The extremely original model, the slightly speckled and thick white glaze, the astoundingly confident use of the material almost at the factory's outset. Only one other example is known, lacking its handle. This, though the handle is broken, fetched £2,835, $7,950 in 1967. In this instance it is unlikely that the condition affected the value of the piece.

A Chelsea strawberry leaf teapot and cover, *circa* 1753-54, Raised Anchor period. There are very few teapots that have survived from this period. Here again the shape is extremely original; the leaf shaped cover and the leaf feet show again the inventiveness of Nicholas Sprimont. This combined with the rarity and early date of the piece has caused teapots of this type to fetch £2,500, $6,000 or more in recent years.

In about 1750, after spending some eighteen months working out new forms and types of decoration, Sprimont started selling porcelain once more. This was the beginning of twenty years of successful production. The opening years, when the mark used was an anchor in relief, are generally referred to as the 'Raised Anchor' period. This merges imperceptibly into the next phase named again after the mark used, the 'Red Anchor'. In these periods the influence of Meissen is felt very strongly throughout the factory's production. The models for figures, as we shall see, were frequently copied. So, too, were the forms of the plates and the shapes of tureens and sauceboats. The manner in which the pieces were decorated, too, shows a debt to the Meissen factory. Around 1745 naturalistic European flower painting became very popular at Meissen. Its foremost exponent was a decorator named Klinger. Many Chelsea plates are decorated in this way. But this debt to Meissen was by no means slavish or lacking in a life of its own. Although some fine shapes, like the peony dish illustrated, show an obvious debt to Meissen, other leaf dishes are of forms peculiar to Chelsea. The Kakiemon bowl, also shown, is obviously derived from a Japanese original, but whether directly or via Meissen one cannot say. Compared with the Meissen Kakiemon bowl it is really a better imitation of the Japanese. The colour of the glaze has been carefully tinged with blue to make it look more like the original, while in the Meissen copy the stark whiteness of the surface is unlike the Japanese original.

A particularly attractive shape which is an entirely Chelsea form is the silver shaped oval dish. This was evolved in the raised anchor period but continues throughout the red anchor as well. These dishes were painted with naturalistic specimen sprays of fruit and flowers. This type of painting is also to be found on large numbers of plates. Many of these were taken from Ehret's illustrations to Miller's book on the flowers from Sir Hans Sloane's garden in Chelsea. Others, exceptionally rare, are painted with American plants. A large number of tea wares, generally octagonal in form, were painted with scenes from Aesop's fables. These are generally associated with the painter Jefferys Hammett O'Neale. He was certainly responsible for one of the factory's productions of the red anchor period, the Warren Hastings service. This has fable scenes in each of the moulded scroll cartouches around the border (see illustration). This form of plate was also used for other services, painted with panels of birds and landscapes.

Tureens formed as pomegranates and other fruit were made at Meissen:

79

Kakiemon octagonal bowl; 17th century.

Meissen octagonal bowl in the Kakiemon style, *circa* 1730, crossed swords marked in blue.

Chelsea octagonal bowl in the Kakiemon style, *circa* 1752, raised anchor mark.

The basic principle is evidently the same in all three of these specimens. However, the Chelsea piece, which is of soft paste porcelain, in contrast to the true porcelain of the other two, is softer and has an appearance of greater depth on the surface. Strangely, though it is a copy, or perhaps even a copy of a copy, the Chelsea piece is at least as expensive as the Meissen copy or the Japanese piece.

Right
A Chelsea oval dish from the Warren Hastings service decorated by J. H. O'Neale. Red Anchor mark. Each of the small scenes round the border is painted with a scene from the fables of La Fontaine. O'Neale painted scenes of this type on smaller pieces, teawares and bowls.
Even a fluted cup and saucer would bring £300—400, $720—950. In 1963 a pair of these dishes fetched £840, $2,350. By 1967 a single example was worth £735, $2,050 at auction.

Top
A pair of peony dishes with Red Anchor marks. These and other similar dishes painted with sunflowers were copies from Meissen and formed stands for sunflower or peony tureens.

A single dish of this type would cost under £150—250, $360—480 today.

but these are rather overshadowed by the variety and brilliance of Chelsea tureens, which were made in the shape of carp, boar's heads, plaice, eels, ducks, rabbits and chicks from the animal world, whilst the garden provided asparagus, melons, apples, pineapples, sunflowers, peonies, cauliflowers and lettuces. Many of the examples found today are marriages between the lid of one and the bottom of another. The majority of these tureens are marked with a red anchor and a number. If the cover and base belong together they

should both bear the same number. These are the most elaborate productions of the red anchor period.

In 1757 Frederick the Great of Prussia defeated the Elector of Saxony, Augustus III. He removed all the workmen from Meissen to Berlin to bolster up his hitherto rather unsuccessful porcelain manufacture. This utterly destroyed Meissen's pre-eminent position and influence in the world of porcelain, which were duly taken over by the Sèvres factory established by Louis XV outside Paris in 1753. By 1770 Meissen had succumbed to the influence of Sèvres: so, too, had Chelsea. The closing phase of the factory's life is known as the 'Gold Anchor' period. This extends from 1760 till 1770 when the factory was taken over by Duesbury of Derby. This period coincided with the height of the Rococo style in Europe and as a result the factory's productions at this time were by far its richest and most elaborate. This richness is largely accounted for by the introduction of gilding, which does not occur in the earlier periods. It coincided also with a wide use of coloured grounds on the dishes and vases. This was obviously inspired by Sèvres, but may, too, have been stimulated by competition from Worcester. The inspiration of Sèvres is acknowledged in 18th century catalogues of Chelsea where the claret ground is described as *Rose Pompadour* and turquoise as *Bleu Céleste*. These two expressions were used at Sèvres to describe pink and turquoise whereas at Chelsea the first describes a colour that can only really be described as claret. The claret ground was often used by itself, or in conjunction with turquoise, which is otherwise very rare. The other major ground colour used at Chelsea was a rich royal blue. This appears at its best and most exuberant in large potpourri vases such as those illustrated. Botanical plates persist into this period, but, as in the example shown, they have gilt rims. New forms included library stands, écuelles copied from Sèvres, chamber candlesticks, and a great variety of shaped vases.

82

A leaf dish with Red Anchor mark. This formed the stand for a melon tureen. Similar dishes were made at Worcester.

Upper right
A pair of mazarine blue pot pourri vases and covers. Gold Anchor period. These particular vases appeared in the sale of 1771, where they are quite clearly described. The mazarine blue grounds and the rich gilding are the typical features of this period of Chelsea, Combined with the panels of figures, which are strongly coloured, and with the vigorous rococo scrollwork of the handles, bases, shoulders and covers, this creates an effect of excessive richness. Vases of this sort were immensely popular in the last century.

In 1965 this pair was sold for £1,100, $3,080. This price, when compared with those paid for the two teapots of the Triangle and Raised Anchor periods highlights the current lack of appreciation for the products of this period.

Right
Three vegetable tureens with Red Anchor marks. The cauliflower is also to be found from Worcester in a similar shape. The apple and the artichoke with their amusing caterpillar and bird finials are good examples of the 'conceits' which were so popular and typical of their day.

Chelsea porcelain has always been expensive to collect, but different periods of the factory's production have been in demand at different times. In the latter half of the last century gold anchor vases (and Sèvres porcelain) were tremendously in vogue. Of all 18th century porcelains they stand out as those that appealed most strongly to the collectors of the Victorian era. They

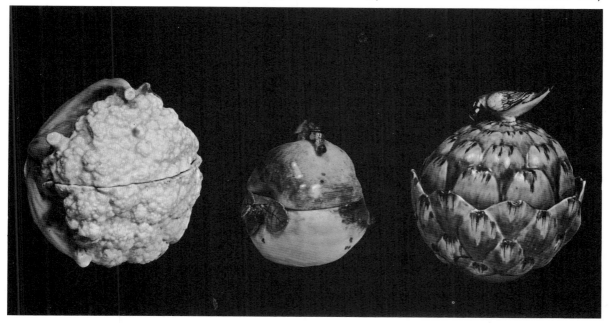

were imbued with a magnificence (almost a vulgarity) which caused fantastic prices to be paid for them. This same quality has in recent years made it extremely difficult to sell them. By comparison with other Chelsea wares they have proved a very bad investment in the past, but the time should soon come when the demand for them may be renewed. The most famous examples of this period are the Chesterfield and Foundling vases. These were bought originally from the factory in 1763 by Dr George Garnier. Just over a century later they were sold at Christie's and purchased by the Earl of Dudley. Even today when increasingly high prices are paid every day for Chelsea and other English factories, such a sum is rarely exceeded. In 1800 the value of the pound was several times what it it today. In 1963, after being lost for half a century they appeared once more on the art market. This time they were sold at a comparative loss, allowing for the cost of depreciation. This is an extreme case; but the trend in fashion it represents has caused a great falling off in the numbers of gold anchor pieces on the market. Those who have acquired or inherited wares of this type have been well advised in retaining them while interest in them recovers. The care and craftsmanship lavished upon them must in due course be appreciated once again.

The red anchor wares have a strong 'blue chip' feeling about them. At the top of the scale there is the Chelsea tureen in china formed as a rabbit, sold by James Christie in December, 1766 for £5. In 1958 the same piece, or a similar one, fetched over £10,000, $24,000, in New York. During the 1950s wares from this period, and figures as we shall see later, were the first seriously to establish themselves as big money-spinners. The vegetable tureens and leaf dishes were objects of great enthusiasm. A pair of asparagus tureens realised 1,400 gns, $3,530 in 1953. This was the time when all other forms of English porcelain were subordinated to Chelsea wares of this type, and every major sale of the time included such pieces. Today, this type of Chelsea is much less seen. Instead it is the raised anchor period, together with all the other pioneering and experimental periods, that is the major centre of interest. As knowledge about the early wares is increased by research their market value seems to appreciate. Chelsea has been expensive for so long that interest in it has tended to suffer from the price. Very few people are able or willing to begin their collecting with an outlay of hundreds of pounds or dollars on one piece. This is indeed a problem; but there are still pieces of fine quality, such as the silver shape dishes, which are decorative without being prohibitively expensive. The same applies to all the Botanical plates which do not fall precisely into the Hans Sloane category.

A Chelsea eel tureen: red anchor marks. One of the most inspired models used at Chelsea and entirely original to the factory.

CHELSEA FIGURES

The production of the English porcelain factories was by no means confined to wares of a more or less utilitarian nature. The majority of them did a large trade in figures. As with the table wares, it was Chelsea which began and remained the foremost exponent. The triangle period did not see the production of many figures: but with the beginning of the 1750's and the managership of Nicholas Sprimont the factory entered on a prolific period of figure

Left

A Meissen figure of Scapin, from the series of Italian comedy figures modelled by J. J. Kändler and P. Rienicke for the Duke of Wiessenfels between 1743 and 1746. The ideas taken from Riccoboni's Histoire du Theatre Italien of 1727 illustrated by Joullain. Today this would fetch £600, $1,440.

Right

A Chelsea figure of Scapin, after the Meissen original illustrated: 4 in. high. Raised Red Anchor mark. From this figure we may reasonably assume that the consignment of figures sent from Dresden included an example of this model. Until 1967 this was an unrecorded model at Chelsea. Two examples then appeared on the market. One fetched £2,940, $8,230, about five times the price of the original Meissen figure, while the other, which was damaged, brough while the other, which was damaged, brought just over a tenth of this price. This shows that rare or unrecorded pieces are still to be found. It also emphasises the difference between a perfect and a damaged piece. *In an Australian Collection*

manufacture. The influence of Meissen, which had manifested itself in the field of table wares, was far more significant in the sphere of figure production. Sir Everard Fawkener, one of Sprimont's patrons, visited Dresden in 1749 and brought back with him examples of figures from the German factory. The majority of these were the work of J. J. Kandler, the great modeller responsible for the larger part of Meissen figures. He was the first to depict the amusing, sometimes grotesque, sometimes pathetic, characters of the Italian comedy in porcelain. He also produced figures of beggars, Chinamen, sportsmen, groups of dancing figures, Turks, and a vast number of birds and animals.

At Chelsea many of Kandler's figures were used as master models for similar examples in soft paste. The Captain from the Italian comedy, The Beggar Musicians, The Dutch Dancers, and various types of Turks (such as those illustrated) echoed in Chelsea porcelain the success they had already enjoyed at Meissen. In general, owing to the method of making the moulds from the original figures, the Chelsea examples are slightly larger than their Meissen counterparts. They are painted in less bold areas of colour and, as opposed to the blue crossed swords mark to be found at the back of Meissen figures of the period, the Chelsea examples bear a very small red anchor mark which is quite often concealed at the figure's feet. The copies from Chelsea are much less common than their Meissen originals.

Of course by no means all the figures made at Chelsea during the raised and red anchor periods owed their form to Meissen originals. Still less did

A Chelsea figure of a duck. Raised Anchor mark (visible on left of tree stump). Taken from pl.100 of G. Edwards: Natural History of Uncommon Birds, published in 1743. Birds of this type are now extremely rare and desirable.

A pair of Chelsea figures of Gardeners with baskets for sweetmeats or flowers. Models in the Meissen style, slightly more massively conceived and less attractive than the two previous figures. This type of figure was very popular earlier in the century.

A Chelsea figure of a Whip-poor-Will or Lesser Goatsucker. Raised Anchor mark (visible on right of tree stump). Taken from pl. 63 of the same book. Both these birds are representatives of a type that has always been popular. They appear very rarely on the market.

Two large Chelsea figures of Seeing and Smelling, one with Red Anchor mark. These form part of a set of the Five Senses. The Chelsea factory was extremely proud of these figures and in the sales in the 18th century each figure was sold as a lot by itself, as: 'A large figure of Seeing' etc. Though great *tours-de-force* they are too massively modelled to appeal to many collectors of Chelsea. The price of these has advanced from £340, $950 each in 1953 to between £1,350 and £1,850, $3,800—5,200 in 1967. These prices are still low compared with the Raised Anchor figure of Scapin which is so much less 'important'.

A Chelsea figure of La Nourrice. Red Anchor Mark. This model derives, unusually, from a French faience original. It appeared originally in the Raised Anchor era and persisted for about eight years. It is one of the finest creations of the Chelsea factory.

Right
A Chelsea group of Mars and Venus. This is transitional between the Red and Gold Anchor periods. The colouring is still broadly handled and the gilding sparingly used. The glaze is thick and definitely glassy with a slightly blue cast. Although a good example of rococo porcelain this group is not of a subject which is much valued.
£315, $760.

A Chelsea figure of a Fishergirl. Another piece of Chelsea modelling at its best. An example of this model fetched £2,250, $6,300 in 1953. It is unlikely that this would fetch significantly more today.

A Chelsea 'Girl-in-a-Swing' factory white figure of a Girl. When Sprimont's partnership with Gouyn was dissolved the workmen from Staffordshire did not return immediately to the Potteries. They set up on their own and produced large numbers of small slip cast scent bottles and seals. They also produced a few figures. Of these the first identified with confidence was a white figure of a girl in a swing, and it is from this that the whole group is named. The porcelain from which the pieces are made differs from that of Chelsea and shows a distinct reaction under ultra-violet. Though the factory is technically much less distinguished than Sprimont's, the highest price paid for English porcelain is for a Girl-in-the-Swing piece.

Left
A Bow group of Harlequin and Columbine. The high scroll base and brightly coloured bocage are typical of Bow in the 1760's. So too is the use of underglaze blue and gilding. The two figures appear in earlier versions separately.

those of the later gold anchor period. There is a great variety of groups and figures which are entirely original in conception. These are extremely rare and thus expensive. The factory made large groups of dancing figures, and Chinese figures which would if sold today be available only to the wealthiest collectors. The same problem arises with the remaining category of figures made in the raised and red anchor periods: the birds. Kandler had a most resounding success with his birds at Meissen. The Chelsea birds were no less brilliant in their quality and execution, and despite the obvious precedent of Meissen the models are entirely new to porcelain and were taken from the illustrations to G. Edwards' *Uncommon Birds* published in 1743. Compared with Meissen birds they are perhaps less crisply formed, but at the same time they are often disconcertingly lifelike. The result is that Chelsea birds are keenly sought after and tend to fetch high prices, as will be seen from the case of the examples illustrated. But even at this comparatively exalted level, there has been appreciation in value over the last decade of several hundred per cent, representing an increase of many thousand-fold over the 18th century price.

The figures and groups of the gold anchor period have recently suffered, in the same way as the other wares of this date. They are much more elaborate than their predecessors of the red anchor era. The plain flat bases of the early figures are replaced by richly gilded scrolls. The intimate scale of the earlier period is lost and often the modelling is massive and the colouring and decoration tend towards the vulgar. Despite these criticisms the quality of the productions, apart from very heavily crazed glaze, is high. The subjects which appear in gold anchor figures are very much less derivative than earlier ones. The debt to Meissen, though still to be felt, is more remote. The majority of the figures were definitely original in conception and ambitious in design. Not all of them achieved an effect which is greatly admired today; but others, notably the magnificent series of Masqueraders and some of the figures of shepherds, sportsmen and sportswomen are fine and attractive.

A pair of Chelsea figures of the Imperial Shepherd and Shepherdess, of the Gold Anchor period. The elaborately scrolled bases and the very picturesque attitudes of the figures are absolutely typical. For many years the modelling of these figures, owing to an impressed R found on some examples, was attributed to Rysbrack the famous sculptor. As a result they were highly valued at the end of the last century. Today a pair of these figures would hardly fetch £500, $1,200.

A small Chelsea figure of David Gabarisco of the Gold Anchor period. An amusing sidelight on the products of the period.

92

So, too, are the candlestick groups which depict the fables of La Fontaine and the small groups of fisherfolk and other tradesmen. These are in strong contrast to large groups, such as the Roman Charity and the series of figures of the Muses, which, although much in demand during the Victorian and Edwardian eras, are now at a discount. For a long time this fall in the public favour affected all figures of the gold anchor period, but there has been a discriminating increase in the value of these pieces, and the smaller, finer examples are probably more highly valued now than they have ever been. Despite this increase, they still stand at a disadvantage beside figures from the earlier periods, and the high prices of the earlier wares are in fact contributing to the revival of appreciation among collectors for gold anchor figures.

A Chelsea figure of a Carpenter. Red Anchor mark clearly visible on the base. The obvious placing for the mark is absolutely typical of Red Anchor figures though it is often smaller than here. The model shows the influence of Meissen and yet the figure is an original conception of the Chelsea factory. This is the most desirable type of Red Anchor figure.

A pair of Chelsea figures of a Shepherd and Shepherdess of the Gold Anchor period. These are much more richly coloured, and in fact more fussy than their predecessors. Gilding plays a much more vital part in the decoration and is indeed used as an integral rather than additional feature.
This pair of figures sold for only £300, $850 in 1965, again strongly in contrast to the prices paid for earlier Chelsea figures.

Bow

BOW WARES

The partnership at Chelsea established the first porcelain factory in London by a short head only. For down in Stratford in the East another factory was set up: Thomas Frye and Edward Heylyn established a factory at Bow (the 'Stratford atte Bow' of Chaucer) in or around 1744. The porcelain they used was the ancestor of our modern bone china, and the proportion of bone ash which it contained is a distinguishing chemical feature of Bow porcelain.

A Bow punchbowl in the *famille rose* style, massively potted in a manner typical of Bow, the colours are thickly enamelled in imitation of the Chinese decoration. The slight discolouration visible on the lip is also a typical Bow trait.

A Bow sauceboat. Another massively potted piece, this exemplifies the robust nature of Bow.
A single sauceboat like this might cost £80, $190 today.

The works were christened ' New Canton '. This was a reference to the centre of the Chinese porcelain industry, for it was at Canton in particular that the wares which were exported to Europe in such quantities were made. Nor does the resemblance end with the name. Chelsea had from the start

A pair of Bow duck tureens and covers. These are very rare and this actual model would seem to be original to the factory, although other duck tureens were made at Chelsea and Meissen.
Today a pair of these might fetch £1,500—£2,000, $3,600—$4,800.

A pair of Bow partridge tureens with red anchor marks. This model was made at Meissen, Bow, Chelsea and Worcester.
Examples from the other factories would probably be more expensive, though this pair might bring over £1,000, $2,400 today.

catered for a sophisticated and wealthy ' West End ' clientele. ' Magnificent services for desart ' were their stock-in-trade. Bow sought to supply a humbler market, although this did not prevent occasional extravaganzas. The bread-and-butter of their trade, then, was blue and white porcelain. This had hitherto been supplied by China, but, as we shall see in a later chapter, soon became a staple English product. Bow was the pioneer in this field as Chelsea did not seriously produce blue and white wares. Compared with Chelsea, Bow lacks a certain quality and style. Where Chelsea is sophisticated, finely potted and modelled, a soft paste imitation of the grandeur of Meissen, Bow is robust and down to earth. It tends to be more massive and its translucency has a yellower character than that of Chelsea. The tone of the lower glaze is softer in appearance. It is less crisply defined and often has a homely gaucheness which does not appear in its more polished rival. Despite, or perhaps because of these basic qualities, the factory did a tremendous amount of business. Its turnover in 1752 amounted to around £50,000 and this does not seem to have been an exceptional year. In general, however, the proprietors of the 18th century porcelain factories made beautiful porcelain but

97

poor profits and like Chelsea the Bow factory was eventually absorbed by William Duesbury in 1770.

The heritage of Bow was the same as that of Chelsea. What they developed from it was different. Meissen and Japan dominated Chelsea in form and decoration. At Bow the foremost influence was Chinese, followed by an interpretation of the styles of other centres which were in turn strongly coloured by the products of Chelsea. The shapes are generally less elaborate than those of Chelsea, though vases and centrepieces were produced in complex forms. The imaginative flights that led to the wide range of tureens of varied shapes and sizes at Chelsea, accompanied by their equally varied and 'conceited' stands, rarely occurred at Bow. The basic shapes are simple; bell-shaped mugs, octagonal plates, plain saucer dishes, robust sauceboats, copied directly from contemporary silver. The appearance of the decoration has more of an 'enamelled' quality than that of Chelsea. This applies particularly, and not surprisingly, to wares of *famille rose* type where the decorators at Bow were trying to imitate contemporary Chinese enamelled porcelains. The copies of Japanese wares are less 'enamelled' in effect, but in their very successful imitations of Chelsea botanical wares the same result can be seen. These pieces also benefit from a great freedom of drawing which is not to be seen on similar Chelsea plates.

Bow is not as glamorous as Chelsea. It is much more a plain man's porcelain, and in general has had a much less record-studded price history. There has been little startling development in the value of Bow over the years, but on the other hand there has been no marked slump. The appreciation has been steady and safe, and pieces of fine quality fetch reasonable prices which, unlike the more speculative figures paid for the products of some factories, are founded on the intrinsic value of the porcelain. Very few Bow wares are really costly: an extensive collection of pieces of good quality could still be formed without ever spending more than about £200 or $500 on a single item and there is little danger of their failing to arouse even more enthusiasm in the future.

BOW FIGURES

Bow figures stand in much the same relation to those produced at Chelsea as do the other wares. They are often similar in inspiration, even derived directly from the same originals, but the modelling is much less sophisticated and at times markedly gauche. This latter characteristic, far from being a defect, is one of the main attractions of Bow figures to many collectors.

The figures of the earliest period, which corresponds broadly to the raised and red anchor periods at Chelsea, have many features in common with their Chelsea contemporaries. In fact many of them were probably derived from Chelsea examples. For the Chelsea potters' system of copying Meissen figures was just as practicable for the potters at Bow and they did not have to go so far for their originals. Thus many of the Meissen models which appear at Chelsea also appear at Bow but in different sizes. The Meissen bases are white and slightly rocky: at Chelsea they are flat and white; while at Bow they tend to be low, circular mounds. The majority of them are unmarked during the early period though some bear an impressed mark resembling a ladder. The decoration of early Bow figures often differs strongly from that used at Chelsea. Many of them would appear to have been decorated outside the factory by William Duesbury (about whom we will hear more when we discuss the Derby factory). The palette used included a distinctive bright but chalky blue and a mauvish pink. Often the clothes have particularly finely painted floral patterns, as in the figure of a Turk illustrated.

Among the early Bow figures there are several which owe no debt to Meissen but are the work of a modeller generally known as the 'Muses Modeller' (because his productions include figures of the Muses). These are on untypical scroll bases with a baroque flavour and should not be confused with the scroll based figures of later periods. Groups of figures from Bow are

A pair of early Bow white Chinoiserie busts, two extremely original models, of which coloured examples can be found. These illustrate very well the white body of the factory's early years.
In 1965: £600, $1,450.

A pair of early Bow figures of a Turk and Companion derived from Meissen originals inspired by the illustrations for the Comte de Ferriol's *Les Nations du Levant*. A later Bow example, with Meissen and Chelsea figures of this model are shown elsewhere. The white bases are typical of early Bow figures, whilst the decoration has the same 'enamelled' appearance that is found on contemporary wares.

A Bow group of the Goddess Kao-mi-Sao. This is one of the factory's most ambitious and successful creations. The progressive increase in the prices paid for examples over the years is indicative of the growing interest in Bow.

Collection: Colonial Williamsburg

A Bow figure of a nun. Nuns, monks and other religious figures are not uncommon at Chelsea, Bow and Longton Hall, all inspired by Meissen. Though extremely fine expressions of the porcelain modellers art they are undervalued when compared with secular figures.

A Bow figure of Smelling from the Five Senses. A fairly unsophisticated version of this theme which is in great contrast with the grandiose interpretation of Chelsea of almost the same date.

rare, though one of the factory's masterpieces is the Chinoiserie group of the Goddess Kao-Mi-Sao illustrated. Pieces such as this are rare and very expensive. The Dutch Dancers of Meissen occur at Bow as well as Chelsea. Animals and birds are also to be found. The majority of them date from the factory's earlier years. The models include pug dogs, a lion and lioness, a Dismal hound and an interesting variety of birds of different types and sizes. While these do not attract the same competition nor therefore the same prices as examples from Chelsea, they are still very desirable and although currently quite expensive, should continue to appreciate.

As the 1750s wore on, the second phase of Bow figures came into being. This, which endured till the factory ceased to exist, is generally called the 'Anchor and Dagger' period. The figures often appear in the same models as those of earlier years (as with the Turk's companion illustrated). The colouring has changed considerably. Underglaze blue, mauve, turquoise and gilding are the dominant tones; the glaze has a bluish cast. The figures are set up on high scroll bases and stand among very spikey coloured bocage. Often in this period figures that had hitherto appeared separately are married into a group. It is generally very obvious that two figures have been placed together rather than conceived as an artistic unity, although in some instances these marriages are very successful. Towards the end of the period the figures became very sloppy and are carelessly made.

By contrast with Chelsea figures those made at Bow never excited the eager competition aroused by gold anchor examples in the last century or by red anchor types in the 1950s. The last fifteen years have seen a steady but accelerating interest, caused partly by the difficulty of obtaining Chelsea figures, a trend which seems unlikely to change.

Three Bow groups from a set of the Seasons. These are examples of the factory's middle period where the gauche modelling is now combined with vigorously moulded scrolls enriched in puce and blue enamel.

BLUE AND WHITE PORCELAIN

The manufacturers of delftware at Bristol, Lambeth and Liverpool reflected in their products the influence of the Chinese blue and white porcelain that arrived in this country in such quantities throughout the 18th century. This influence, however, is shown far more by the porcelain manufacturers at Worcester, Bow, Liverpool, Lowestoft, Derby, Longton Hall, Plymouth and Chelsea.

Decoration in underglaze blue involves hardly any more skill or expense than the production of plain white glazed wares, and most of the pieces of this type were produced for ordinary household use. In fact, had not Josiah Wedgwood perfected the production of creamware, we might still use blue and white wares for household purposes to this day. Blue and white ware had been attempted at Meissen earlier in the century; but they were not very

A Worcester blue and white 'Cabbage Leaf' jug. Blue crossed swords mark. This is a fairly early example of a very successful Worcester invention which, with the addition of a mask spout was produced for many years at Worcester and then at Caughley. The later versions are quite common but this earlier type is less easy to find, though still not expensive.
£55, $135.
7¼ in. high.

successful with the colour of the blue. The scale and success of the production in England was quite unequalled in Europe and therefore this aspect of English ceramic manufacture represents a peculiarly interesting contribution to the history of porcelain. It is also the area of porcelain manufacture in England where the influence of Chinese wares dominates, to the virtual exclusion of earlier or contemporary European products. Although eight factories at least produced blue and white porcelains, Bow and Worcester were the major producers and the other factories, with the exception of Chelsea, were inspired and closely influenced by these centres. Chelsea was not a serious producer of blue and white and only a very few pieces survive. These are disproportionately expensive and only rarely appear on the market.

The Bow wares combine an unequivocal usefulness with slightly naive decoration. Like the coloured wares and the figures, Bow blue and white is robustly potted. The wares of the earlier years, up to the early 1760's, are those of the best quality, and, as with the later figures, those of the factory's closing years are not very distinguished. While Worcester is perhaps more varied in the forms to be found in its blue and white, the variety of flat wares produced at Bow was tremendous. It was this aspect of the factory's output which made it the most successful in Europe and the most serious competitor with the Chinese blue and white wares by which it was inspired. Almost all the decoration to be found on Bow wares is of Oriental origin. Scenes with pagoda buildings in landscapes, flowering plants on terraces, and other such subjects are the backbone of the Bow painter's repertoire. Some pieces occur with transfer printed decoration such as may also be found in greater quantities at Worcester. Others, rarer still, may be found bearing dates or inscriptions comparable with those on delftwares and later on, Lowestoft. Another typical feature of Bow decoration in blue and white is the powder-blue ground, again copied from Chinese wares. Characteristic specimens have fan shaped reserves with Oriental scenes. Despite the prodigious volume of blue and white that Bow must have produced, only a limited quantity survives, and to collect it would require time and patience, although it would not necessarily prove very expensive.

A Worcester blue and white oval sauceboat. An attractive combination of good Chinese decoration and fine moulding.
£55—65, $135—155.
5 in. wide.

The volume of Worcester wares available to would-be collectors is perhaps greater than that of Bow. However, of these the majority are transfer printed tea-wares with conspicuously little variety in quality or design over a period of fifteen years. The pieces with painted decoration are immensely varied and of good quality, particularly those from Lund's factory at Bristol, and from the early years at Worcester. The blue and white wares of Worcester occur in a large number of different forms. In fact most of the shapes found in the coloured wares, and some beside, are to be seen in blue and white. The fine potting which typifies all Worcester porcelain extends even to the overtly useful blue and white wares. The double lipped sauceboats are classic examples of this. There are many distinct Oriental patterns to be found on Worcester blue and white, but all of them share a vitality and originality in their interpretation of Oriental themes. These are combined with forms which are much more adventurous than those at Bow and tend to belie the useful nature of the wares. The best of these pieces are the sauceboats. Flat wares in blue and white rarely occur at Worcester, and of those the majority are transfer-printed.

The production of blue and white at Derby could only be called large when compared with that of Chelsea. Pieces from Derby are therefore not easy to find. The blue is far brighter than that of Bow or Worcester, and the designs and forms tend to be closely similar to, if not direct imitations of Worcester. The transfer printed designs, and indeed the whole technique of transfer-printed decoration were brought from Worcester by Richard Holdship and it was he who was responsible for its execution at Derby. Many of the Derby forms, when not derived from Worcester, are similar to those found in contemporary coloured wares, and many bear the patch marks so typical of Derby figures of the period.

Collectors in the south of England or in the United States will find it extremely difficult to find pieces of Derby blue and white. The same problem applies to collecting Lowestoft or wares from the various Liverpool factories. The factory at Lowestoft was established in 1757. The ware was developed

A Ralph Wood Toby jug. This is an absolutely standard Toby which differs from the next solely in the quality of the decoration. This type is much less valuable than the rarer examples such as Martha Gunn, the Squire, Lord Vernon and other jugs derived from contemporary figures.

A Worcester finger bowl stand: workman's mark TF. An example of the cormorant pattern, one of the finest early Worcester designs on blue and white china.
With its bowl this would be an extremely valuable piece. Without it it still fetched £115, $276 as opposed to £38, $105 some four years ago.
6 in. diameter.

In an American collection

from experiments carried out at Bow, and the links between the two factories are very strong. Most Lowestoft pieces are to be found in East Anglia and a study must be made of the major public collections in that area. This factory produced many more pieces with inscriptions than the others so far described. In fact the Lowestoft potters equalled those at the delft factories in their enthusiasm for inscribed and dated pieces of a commemorative nature. A speciality was the circular birth tablets, while several of the inscribed pieces were evidently intended as souvenirs for the towns' visitors.

Apart from these freely decorated wares Lowestoft also produced transfer-printed wares. To the confusion of the student and collector, Lowestoft too used the designs which were originated at Worcester, though of course the pieces on which they appear differ in shape. So too do the wares from the Liverpool blue and white factories. These factories, of which there were several, produced many wares that appear like poor examples of Worcester. This applies particularly to the Chaffers factory, which was, with William Reid's, one of the first. Both were established in about 1754, though production is unlikely to have started at either before the following year. Chaffers employed Richard Podmore, formerly a workman at Worcester, so it is scarcely surprising that a similarity exists between the products of the two places.

The presence in Liverpool of the printing establishment of Messrs. Sadler & Green, also explains the very high proportion of wares with transfer-printed decoration, in sepia, black and blue. The output of the Liverpool factories has a rather more practical note than that of Worcester. Tureens and dinner wares are more common, so are chamber candlesticks, and other forms not found at Worcester. William Ball's factory was responsible for what is probably the largest piece of English blue and white porcelain, if not porcelain of any sort, a large 'potiche' and cover, evidently of oriental inspiration. Longton Hall also produced wares in blue and white, generally very similar in form to the pieces to be found with coloured decoration. The Plymouth hard paste factory, too, made blue and white wares, and many of these are in

A pair of Worcester blue and white wall pockets. These should be compared with the coloured examples shown elsewhere. The trailing flowering branches are again a feature of early blue and white decoration at Worcester.

Right
A pair of Worcester blue and white wall pockets. These more elaborate models are somewhat later than the simpler ones above. The same form may also be found in saltglaze. Since these pieces are virtually impossible to display in cabinets and have to be hung around the room, they do not command the prices their elaborate nature would seem to warrant.

In an American collection

A Liverpool blue and white bowl. It has not been definitely established which of the Liverpool factories was responsible for this piece. The contour of the bowl is quite unlike that of a Worcester one, though the quality of the decoration is on a level with early Worcester painting. The deep footrim is also to be compared with the usual Worcester one which is shallower and more triangular in cross section. The actual surface that touches the ground is fairly flat.

In an American collection

A Worcester blue and white triple shell sweetmeat dish. These were made at Derby, Bow and Plymouth as well. The present example is a fairly simple one. Some specimens, particularly those from Bow, have three or even four tiers of shells.

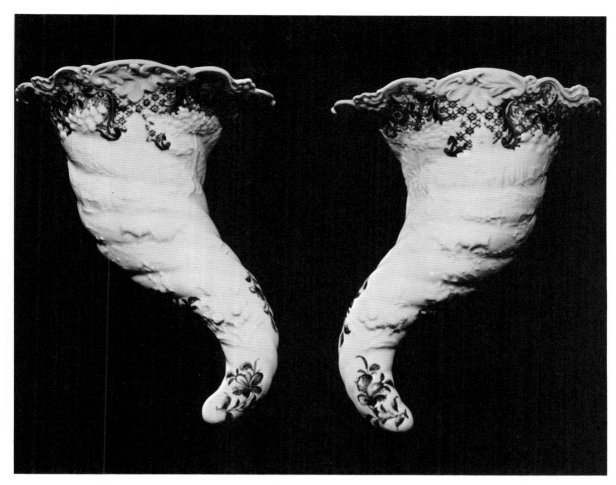

shapes that were made earlier at Worcester or Longton Hall: nor does the decoration show great innovation.

It was not long ago that blue and white wares, not only in English porcelain, but also in English delft and Chinese porcelain, were scarcely regarded at all. They were treated as an interesting adjunct to the more colourful wares and figures, but were not seriously collected on a large scale. Even five years ago

the attention given to them had not reached great proportions; but in 1963 the publication of Dr Bernard Watney's book *English Blue and White Porcelain of the 18th century* gave fresh impetus to a gradually increasing interest. It also set down a great deal of information without which the beginner would find the study and collection of blue and white porcelain very much harder. Although blue and white porcelain is not the most sophisticated class of production, nor the most expensive to collect, it is the most difficult sphere in which to achieve a confident knowledge, and in which to attribute wares to one factory or another with any measure of certainty. It can be fairly said that the expert in blue and white wares will also be competent to distinguish the more highly decorated wares of one factory from those of another. However, it is possible to tell the coloured wares of, say, Worcester from those of Chelsea or Bow, and yet experience the greatest difficulty in distinguishing the blue and white wares of the various centres. Thus blue and white provides a very good starting ground for the collector. Not only does it form a comparatively cheap way of beginning, but it also gives a good training in the study of porcelain. This is why, perhaps, it has attracted so much attention recently.

The current attention does not, of course, extend indiscriminately over all blue and white wares to the same degree. Futhermore, the pieces with painted decoration are, in general, more desirable than those that are transfer-printed, although some printed pieces have rare patterns which enhance their interest. The type of decoration on the painted pieces has a radical influence on the value. The combination of unusual painting with a form rare in blue and white is evidently the most sought after; but even then a minute percentage of the numerous pieces of blue and white that are sold each year fetch much more than £50, $120, while many quite attractive specimens cost less. The best course for the collector to adopt, in this sphere in particular, is to view sales containing blue and white wares and watch the prices realised by the various types. He may not remain a blue and white collector for long, but it will certainly provide a good training and it is extremely unlikely that such a collector will fail to show a good short term appreciation.

WORCESTER

The pre-eminence of Chelsea on the attention of the modern collector has suffered a strong challenge from the greatest of the factories outside London. Worcester, the largest of the provincial centres, was certainly in existence by 1752, but by a strange anomaly the business was originally founded at Bristol, where it was located in a building known as Lowdin's or Lund's china works. The Worcester factory had an extremely varied and prolific output, and in this case, unlike that of the London establishments at Bow and Chelsea, the end of the period brought not financial decline but a change of style. This adaptability, which was again noticeable at the beginning of the 19th century, has kept the factory in production to this date.

The Bristol-Worcester heritage differed from that of the metropolitan factories. The association with Bristol placed at the disposal of the Worcester porcelain manufacturers the artistic and technical skill of the delft potters. Perhaps the provincial situation of the factory deprived it of the tremendous impact of the German porcelain which was so clearly felt in London. On the other hand, ships were docking regularly at Bristol with huge loads of china from Canton. Blue and white porcelains tended to be generally in demand throughout the provinces while every larger house was acquiring enamelled table wares from both China and Japan. The blue and white wares inspired by this influx fall into the scope of another chapter; but the coloured products of the Worcester factory are generally collected and considered independently of them. The coloured wares from the Lund's Bristol-early-Worcester period have an enamelled surface of which the illustrated cream jug is typical. Typical, too, of Worcester as a whole is the shape, with the shallow moulded scrolls reminiscent of the chasing on rococo silver. The scroll form of the handle also derives from the work of the contemporary silversmith.

The paste used at Bristol and at Worcester is soft and similar to that used at the London factories but with the addition of soaprock or steatite. The translucency has a definite green quality while the glaze, which has a bluish tinge, has a tendency to retract around the base within the foot rim leaving an unglazed area. On the flat pieces the centre has a tendency to drop slightly.

An early Worcester sauceboat. This hexagonal silver shape was used at Lund's Bristol factory. It also occurs bearing the mark Wigornia (the Latin name for Worcester). The shape of the handle is most felicitous. The enamelled floral border is to be found on several pieces of this date. £80, $196.

The porcelain of the first or 'Wall' period, so called because Dr Wall was one, although not the most prominent, of the thirteen partners, was particularly finely potted. The majority, but by no means all, of the pieces bear the Wall mark, a fretted square in blue, while others are marked with a crescent in blue. The decoration at the factory falls, broadly, into seven categories; Chinese decoration, Japanese decoration, European flowers, pencilled wares, armorial pieces, coloured grounds, and transfer-printed wares. Some pieces fall into two of these categories at once.

The coloured grounds are in general the most sought after. Of these the most common is the blue scale pattern, while apple green, claret, yellow, pink and turquoise are comparatively rare. Pieces of this type are normally found

A pair of *gros-bleu* oviform vases and covers with blue Square Seal marks, *circa* 1765. These are painted with panels of exotic birds within gilt rococo scroll-work cartouches entirely typical of Worcester.

with panels of decoration enclosed by gilt borders or cartouches. These, which are generally formed from scrolls and sprays of flowers in the contemporary rococo taste, are reminiscent in shape of contemporary mirrors and vases and are thus referred to as vase and mirror shaped cartouches. The decoration that occupies the panels is in its turn varied. Simple bouquets of flowers are fairly common with scale blue, apple green and yellow. A variant to be found with scale blue is a pattern of swags of flowers continuing through all the panels. Fairly common, too, with the scale blue are designs of Oriental inspiration such as the Ho-Ho bird and Jabberwocky patterns. Rarer pieces are painted with fruit and exotic birds. These last two types of decoration can also be found on the apple green, claret and yellow grounds. Exceptionally pieces occur with figure subjects or fable scenes after Barlow's Edition of Aesop's Fables, but these seldom fall within the scope of the ordinary collector.

Generally, the scale blue and apple green grounds occur on flat wares, teapots, jugs, and cups and saucers; the shapes are simple, apart from the leaf dishes. Also found are vases, which were made in matching pairs.

The pencilled wares were peculiar to Worcester. They are not very common but appeal only to a limited number of collectors. Most, like the saucer dish illustrated, show a Chinese inspiration. The drawing is usually in black and so lacks the colour which is required by the majority of porcelain collectors, though the puce decorated pieces are extremely attractive.

Polychrome decoration of Chinese inspiration is comparatively easy to find among Worcester wares. Figure subjects, usually ladies among vases of flowers on tall stands, are often to be seen on teawares and leaf dishes. Oriental landscapes also occur on some early pieces. Fairly frequent too are pieces decorated in an imitation of contemporary *famille rose*, pieces with panels of figures on elaborately gilt scroll pattern grounds with lesser landscape vignettes.

The influence of Japanese porcelain, particularly the Imari rather than the Kakiemon wares, was equally strong, though freely interpreted. Often pieces of this sort bear a pseudo-Chinese character mark in blue on the back. The decoration usually consists of ' Japanese ' polychrome panels divided by

115

radiating blue bands which are in turn reserved with floral medallions. Most Worcester wares of this type are not conspicuous for their quality or interest, but fine specimens can be very attractive.

Besides those pieces inspired by Japanese porcelain there are also wares made as replacements for Chinese and Japanese services, in which cases the original decoration is minutely copied. Since this was often done for only a few pieces of a particular pattern, specimens of this sort are very rare and

Two lobed oval dishes with blue Crescent marks, *circa* 1765. The shape is a typical Worcester one. The dish on the left painted with bouquets of flowers in pure monochrome, the blue border with gilt enrichment. The right hand dish painted by the 'Spotted Fruit Painter' with bunches and baskets of fruit. The shaped *gros-bleu* border shows the influence of Sèvres in its *caillouté* gilding.
£75 and £200, $180 and $480.

Left
A yellow ground junket dish, *circa* 1765. The bouquets of flowers in colours, the moulded cartouches puce and the basketwork ground yellow.
Brilliant examples have fetched up to £1,250, $3,000.

A coffee cup and saucer pencilled in puce.

Right
A black pencilled saucer dish. A most charming example of Chinoiserie decoration, full of the spirit of Chinese Chippendale.
£105, $295 (1965).

varied. The decoration in these cases was often quite untypical of the usual run of Worcester decoration in the Oriental style. The Chinese enamellers in Canton did a particularly successful business in services enamelled with the coats-of-arms of families both in this country and on the Continent. At Worcester they imitated the Chinese in this as in other ways and produced their own armorial wares. They are not very common nor are they perhaps as successful in their artistic effect as their Oriental equivalents. However, they are comparatively rare and no collection of Worcester can be regarded as complete without an example of this type.

European flowers on a plain white ground such as were used at all the major English and European factories were frequently employed as a decorative motif at Worcester. The quality of the painting on pieces of this type varies immensely and some of it is very ordinary. Other pieces, such as the tea bowl and saucer illustrated, are remarkably fine. There are also examples decorated with landscape scenes and rococo scroll cartouches, as in the leaf jug shown.

The spirit of the rococo is also felt in another major class of Worcester wares, those with transfer-printed decoration. This was a major technical breakthrough in the production of decorated porcelain. The process of transfer printing on enamels from copper plates was discovered in the early 1750's at Battersea. The similar discovery at Worcester, although almost contemporary, appears to have been quite independent. Richard Holdship and Robert Hancock discovered that a design, printed by an engraved copper block on a sheet of paper, could be transferred from that paper on to an unglazed piece of porcelain. These transfer prints were produced in fairly large numbers, most often in sepia or underglaze blue, but sometimes in lilac and iron red. The majority of the designs can be attributed to Robert Hancock: several pieces are in fact signed R. H., Worcester at the bottom of the design. Among these are the mugs portraying Frederick the Great between martial trophies, Masonic pieces and numerous teawares (each transfer-printed with a wide variety of pastoral subjects), Chinoiserie scenes and landscapes. Owing to

A black pencilled oval sauce boat, *circa* 1755-8. A superb example of modelling. This piece sold in 1967 for £85, $238, and brought £126, $302 in 1968.

the fact that pieces had generally room for at least two, and in the case of jugs and mugs sometimes three, different printed subjects, and since the same prints do not always appear together, countless permutations of transfer patterns are found. The subjects that do occur have been noted, but there is always the chance that some unrecorded design will appear to enhance the established corpus. A further interesting development, to be found on pieces transfer-printed in lilac (in particular those with designs of ruined classical buildings in landscapes) is the addition of decoration in colours. The effect of this, though unexpected, can be most successful.

The skill and effort of the Worcester factory was to the greatest extent concentrated on useful wares. Teawares and dessertwares were made in most of the major groups discussed above. Vases were also made in fairly large numbers; but these are overshadowed today by the baskets which the factory produced in a variety of forms and with several different forms of decoration. They range from plain circular baskets, through circular two handled examples, oval baskets with and without handles, and culminate in the chestnut baskets. These were one of the factory's most original creations. Each basket has handles formed as flowering branches, so too the oval quatrefoil stands and the pierced covers. All the forms of basket are to be found in blue and white, and occur with scale blue, yellow and claret grounds, or with fruit or

Examples of transfer printing on cups and saucers. The central group decorated in enamel colours over a lilac coloured transfer.

118

A transfer printed jug, decorated in black with a Chinese scene.

A transfer printed punch bowl, *circa* 1770, with hunting scenes after originals by James Seymour.

A saucer dish with lilac transfer landscape. This is the only piece recorded with this print.
In 1965 this was sold for £38, $106, and in 1968 it brought

flowers. A combination of scale blue and yellow grounds is also known, as in the example illustrated.

Worcester also produced tureens, generally copied from those made at Chelsea or Meissen. Partridge tureens were made at Bow, Chelsea and Worcester, but many of those not made at Chelsea bear red anchor marks. Worcester pieces often bear fictive Chinese character marks while others, generally pieces of better quality, bear the crossed swords of the Meissen factory accompanied by the number 6. Cauliflower tureens were also frequently produced, and the least common of these bear transfer-printed decoration.

Where Chelsea, Bow, Derby and Longton Hall all made numerous figures of different sorts, at Worcester they were produced in almost negligible quantities. In fact it was for many years believed that none were made, and even those who thought they had been were unable to identify any examples positively. Only last year (1967) a hitherto unknown 'Birds in Branches' group has been identified, raising the number of known models from six to seven. Of these the finest are the pair of Turks, whilst the gardeners and the sportsmen, the other known figures, have a gaucheness to them which reminds one of the Bow style. Some of the examples stand on high scroll bases not unlike those found at Bow during the later period. The explanation of this is that the modeller who was most probably responsible, a Mr Tebo, was, until his arrival at Worcester in the late 60's, an employee at the Bow factory. He went on from Worcester to the hard paste factory at Bristol in 1772. A few undecorated specimens of the figures are known, but the majority are coloured.

Anyone beginning to collect Worcester porcelain would clearly not be able to start by collecting figures. In the first place they are in very short supply and while single specimens do occur on the market from time to time, a matching pair is only obtainable at vast expense. The table wares and vases appear very frequently. Of these the pieces with coloured grounds are the objects of the most attention. Yellow is the most sought after and appears to be appreciating in value. In 1945 a complete yellow tea service painted with panels of birds fetched £500, a remarkable price at the time. When the teapot from this same service reappeared at auction in the autumn of 1965 with its

120

A white figure of a Gardener. One of the rare Worcester figures produced between 1768 and 1772.

A coloured example of this figure fetched over £1,700, $4,080 in 1968: a white one would bring about £500, $1,200.

Tea caddy and cover of the Sir Joshua Reynolds pattern. The covers of the caddies are unfortunately prone to being lost, so those examples with their original covers are all the more rare. This one is also unusual in that it is fluted.

In 1968 this fetched £400, $960 but many tea caddies should be available for less.

A pair of early Worcester wall vases, *circa* 1755, formed as cornucopias and painted with flower sprays in colours. These are also to be found in blue and white. Since they do not fit easily into cabinets they are not liked by many collectors and are proportionately less highly valued than other pieces that may be less interesting but are simpler to accomodate.

121

A tea bowl and saucer decorated by James Rodgers, *circa* 1760. An example of brilliant flower painting such as is not found on the wares decorated at the factory, and is only equalled by the products of the Giles workshop in Camden Town.

In 1967 a pair of these tea bowls and saucers brought £252, $605.

A pair of Worcester figures of Turks. These were probably modelled by Tebo during his short stay at Worcester between 1768 and 1770. Figures from Worcester are rare, but they are even less easy to find in pairs. In 1965 this pair fetched £2,520, $7,060. In 1968 the Gardener's Companion alone fetched £1,750, $4,200.

A Worcester blue scale and yellow ground chestnut basket cover and stand. This form is to be found in blue and white, blue scale, with yellow ground and with Giles decoration. This present decoration, though perhaps the rarest of all, is more rare than beautiful. In 1967 this fetched almost £1,000, $2,800 when a blue and white example fetched £250, $700.

hexagonal stand, it fetched over £4,000, $9,600. This vast price was largely caused by its being the only known specimen. However, other yellow ground pieces have made considerable, albeit smaller, gains in value over the same period. The same tendency is to be observed in the sphere of apple green wares. Of these one tankard fetched £45 when sold at Christie's in 1938. In 1966 it realised 1,400 gns, $3,530. Another, slightly larger, brought £1,800, $4,320 in the autumn of 1965.

The immense interest and prices generated by the more glamorous pieces has had a contagious effect on the majority of the more ordinary wares. Admittedly some sectors are still a little neglected, but in view of the current cost of the other wares, they must soon receive more attention from collectors of Worcester. The most likely types are pieces with Chinese decoration and the pencilled wares. The transfer-printed pieces, in conjunction with transfer-printed enamels from Battersea and Birmingham and creamware and porcelain from Liverpool have recently been the objects of intensive research. As a result the market in them has been particularly firm and would seem set fair to continue so. It is still necessary to study which designs are the uncommon ones, and which colours the rarer.

Fundamentally the reason for the popularity of Worcester lies in its strong decorative qualities. It is ornamental and distinguished. The gilding never reaches the opulence of gold anchor Chelsea, but it does impart a feeling of richness to the porcelain while often setting off the colour grounds to great advantage. Another factor may be that, whereas the glaze of late red anchor and gold anchor wares at Chelsea show a tendency towards crazing or even discolouration, the appearance of most Worcester pieces today is much the same as when they left the factory two centuries ago.

The products of Worcester present a wide variety of choice for the collector. There is an infinite variety of patterns to be found, some fairly common, others extremely rare. Although some of the pieces, in particular the finer specimens, with pink, yellow, apple green and scale blue grounds, are now very expensive, the vast majority of pieces still can be acquired for under £200, $500, though of course there is an increasing tendency for the more interesting and unusual specimens to fetch prices beyond this level.

A Chelsea Figure of a Barn Owl. Raised Anchor Period. Only four of these figures are recorded. One of them fetched £900, $2,520 in 1956. Ten years later this one bought £4,200, $11,760. The remaining two are in museums. The paste shows the typical characteristics of the Raised Anchor Period.

THE WORK OF JAMES GILES

A Coalport dessert service: this typifies the
opulence of Regency decoration on table
wares at its best. The combination of
brilliantly coloured fruit in the centres with
rich gilding at the borders shows the
technical proficiency of the potters of the
day.

For many years collectors and experts were perplexed by the fact that pieces undoubtedly of Worcester and Chelsea manufacture appeared to be decorated by the same hand. Similar examples from Bow cropped up from time to time. The majority of these pieces were painted with exotic birds with brilliant, though rather dishevelled, plumage, or with cut fruit. Examples also occur with decoration in green lake and with claret grounds. Evidently an independent decorator was at work on both Chelsea and Worcester porcelain. For a long time it was thought probable that he could be identified as James Giles, who had a decorating shop in Camden Town and retail premises in Cockspur Street, Soho. Recently the Auctioneer's catalogue of the sale in which his entire stock-in-trade was dispersed came to light at Christie's, while his sales ledger was produced by one of his descendants some thirty-five years ago. These documents have revealed in some detail what wares Giles dealt in. They included glass as well as porcelains, both English and German.

Eighteenth century catalogues and ledgers tend, alas, to be unspecific in just those points which students today are most anxious to clarify. Yet in this case they do make it clear that by no means all of Giles's stock-in-trade was decorated in his workshop. He was a prominent buyer at Duesbury's Chelsea-Derby sales which took place, also in Christie's sale rooms in Pall Mall, in the early 1770's. However, he also bought parcels of porcelains direct from Duesbury and in the white from the Worcester factory. Some pieces he bought from Worcester with blue scale decoration but without the painting in the panels or gilding. There is no way of telling whether the claret grounds found on both Worcester and Chelsea pieces decorated by Giles were enamelled in the factories or in his studio. The basis for attribution of pieces to Giles's atelier is founded on comparison with glass known to have emanated from Giles's workshop and on a few plates that were handed down to his descendants. Other pieces, such as the teapot illustrated, can definitely be ascribed to the Giles workshop. We can find a tea service which answers the same description in Giles's sale catalogue (Lot 230 on the third of the five days of sale). The description in 1774 reads: ' a compleat tea-service ribb'd, 41 pieces, to beautiful fancy striped pattern '. The service on that occasion sold for

A Worcester plate decorated in Giles' workshop decorated in extremely clear and fluid colours with sprays of flowers. This type of painting is to be found on plates given to the Victoria and Albert Musuem by Giles' descendants.
7 in. diameter.
£170, $410.

A Worcester white and gold tea pot and cover gilt in Giles' workshop. Until quite recently this type of decoration was not associated with Giles' atelier. However there are pieces of opaque glass to be found with similar decoration and Christie's sale of James Giles stock-in-trade contains pieces which answer the same description:- 'Lot 43, on the 4th day of sale, a complete tea service elegantly painted in gold with stags heads, pateras, festoons of husks, etc.' White and gold pieces never command prices comparable with coloured wares and examples such as this, though an essential aspect of Giles decoration, should not prove expensive.
7 in. wide.

A Worcester plate painted with Cut Fruit and Insects. This particular type of decoration is associated with a painter called 'The Cut Fruit Painter'. It also occurs on services with claret and turquoise grounds and on Chelsea porcelain.
£170, $410.
7¼ in. diameter.

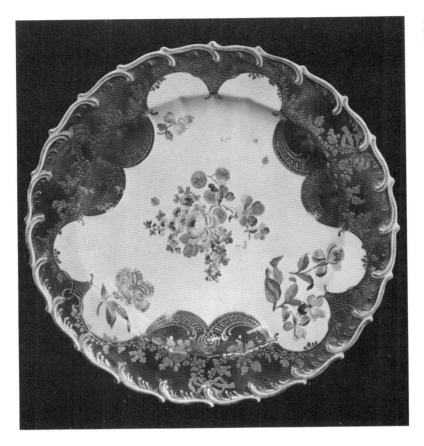

A Chelsea claret ground plate with Giles decoration from the gold anchor period. The flower painting by the same hand as the Worcester plate shown. The claret border richly gilt and edged with turquoise and gold. Pieces like this are also clearly described in the Giles sale where they sold for a few shillings each.
In 1967 they fetched about £250, $600 each. 9 in. diameter.

A Bow plate decorated in the Giles workshop. This appears far more like a Chelsea piece of the Gold Anchor period than Bow. The birds are the same as those on the Worcester dish illustrated whilst the flower painting is similar to that on Chelsea and Worcester pieces painted in the Giles workshop. Bow porcelain with Giles decoration is much rarer than Chelsea or Worcester but less valued by collectors.

£18. 18. 6: today a single cup and saucer of this pattern fetches £120. The decoration is most unusual for Worcester, with vertical stripes in claret and turquoise and with ciselé gilt swags. The same gilding, and combination of colours occurs on the oval dish illustrated, which is a typical piece of Chelsea porcelain bearing the gold anchor mark. The gilding is similar in quality to that visible on the teapot, the flowers in the central field displaying many characteristics to be found on Worcester and on glassware. It once formed part of a service which answers excellently to the description of lot 57 on the third day: ' a most superb and elegant desert service fine crimson border and richly finished with gold viz 3 dozen of plates and 20 dishes and compoteers of different sizes '. Some of the finest Worcester baskets, too, are those which bear Giles decoration. Examples are to be found with cut fruit and with floral painting on a blue scale ground.

The bird decoration done in Giles's workshop has to be distinguished very carefully from that found on pieces of Chelsea and Worcester decorated at the factories. The birds of Giles always have a distinctly dishevelled appearance and were evidently painted with much greater freedom than their counterparts produced at the factories. Giles decorated wares are, of course, a limited field. They form, as it were, subsections of Chelsea and Worcester, and tend to be of finer quality: this, combined with the small extent of his output as compared with that of the two major factories has led to Giles ware becoming, and remaining, very much a ' blue chip ' in English porcelain. The bright light of research has also played a leading part in stimulating interest in the production of this outside enameller, although it has tended only to confirm suspected attributions. Above all things the quality of the decoration, in particular of the rich honey gilding, sets Giles's work on Worcester and Chelsea well above the wares decorated at the factories themselves.

A Worcester yellow ground basketwork dish decorated in the Giles atelier. The combination of the most desirable ground colour, yellow, with the most sought after decoration, that of Giles' workshop has resulted in some extremely high prices for wares of this class.

This one sold for £1,995, $5,700 in 1965. Another in 1957 fetched 560 guineas, $1,725. In 1946 a yellow ground tea service of this type brought £500, $1,400. In 1965 the teapot, cover and stand of this same service was sold for £4,200, $11,750.

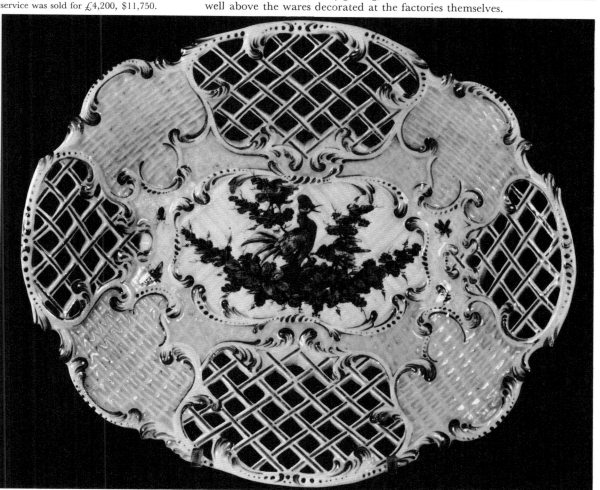

DERBY, LONGTON HALL, PLYMOUTH, BRISTOL

The last of the major factories to start was that at Derby, set up by John Heath and Andrew Planché. The work of this period of the factory's production was small, and information about it not clear. The majority of the pieces produced would seem to have been figures. These have many affinities with contemporary Bow and Chelsea examples. The influence of Meissen is less conspicuous here than at the London factories. The bases of the earliest figures are simply rounded like those of Bow; but the glaze recedes from the edges in a manner peculiar to this period of Derby. As a result they are known as 'dry edge' figures. The modelling is original and lively, displaying at all times a sensitive use of the material. The best examples of this are the Chinoiserie groups and figures, which display the mastery the factory's modellers had so quickly achieved over their medium. Shepherds and Shepherdesses appear like sophisticated pieces of Bow. Animals were also produced, notably wild boars and leopards, both in models original to Derby. The factory also made birds, though these only rarely rise to the heights of Chelsea or even of Bow.

An early Derby oval basket, with yellow ground. Compared with those from Chelsea or Worcester, baskets from Derby are rare. This one, with a figure subject and yellow ground, is an exceptional example.

In 1755 the management of the factory was taken over by William Duesbury. Duesbury, who had operated a decorating shop in London, had been responsible for the decoration of early Derby and Bow porcelains. He was to become the Josiah Wedgwood of the English porcelain world. His highly successful factory eventually absorbed both the great London factories. Unfortunately perhaps, his financial success was achieved at the price of quality and originality. His figures were made in very large numbers. The models include Diana, Minerva, Athene, Venus and Cupid, Mars and Brittania from the Pantheon; shepherds and shepherdesses and gardeners in many varieties. Sets of the Continents and the Seasons were successful, though made in fairly large numbers. The Seasons took their inspiration from Meissen, but,

134

unlike the figures of Bow and Chelsea, the models from which they were taken, were not by J. J. Kändler but a later modeller J. F. Eberlein. The Continents appear in continuing editions till the end of the century. The figures of the 1760's are typified by scroll bases, generally enriched in turquoise and gold. The figures often stand before flowering trees or 'bocage' such as is also to be found on Bow figures of the same date. The bases often show three circular masks underneath, known as 'patch' marks and caused by the pads of damp clay on which the figures stood in the kiln. Although some examples of this period are fine, many of the Derby figures are rather disappointing.

The merger with Chelsea and the removal of the moulds from the factory to Derby opened up a new period in the factory's history. Biscuit, white unglazed porcelain wares and groups were made. Among these, vases of flowers in the Adam taste were particularly successful, though these are not common. The groups and figures depict classical nymphs and cupids, shepherds and shepherdesses. Similar coloured groups also occur. These are

An early Derby figure of a boar. This is an original Derby model which is not found at the other factories. It is more commonly found in white with its companion. a recumbent boar copied from the famous Porcellino in Florence.

generally decorated in pale colours with yellow, green, buff and pink dominant. They have the model number incised under the base which is frequently partly glazed. Several groups from the previous decades also recur, brought up to date. New models were also added to the repertoire. Typical of these are figures on rectangular bases with canted corners, the bases thinly potted and hollow.

Until comparatively recently (the 1930's) the greater part of the earlier productions of Derby were attributed to Chelsea. This arose partly from the confusion caused by Duesbury's takeover of Chelsea and partly from the lack of documentary evidence about the Derby factory. As a result many of the fairly ordinary figures of the 1760's, Milton, Shakespeare, the Ranelagh Dancers and others were vastly prized as Chelsea and will be found in all old

135

A pair of early Derby figures. Like contemporary Bow figures these stand on circular white bases, but they are slightly more modelled than at Bow. Blue-green, yellow and pink are the most prominent colours.

A set of Derby figures of the Four Seasons, copied from Meissen originals modelled by J. F. Eberlein. The low scroll bases date these around 1760. Green, yellow and lilac are again prominent colours.
A complete set would cost £600—800, $1,450—1,900, though any single figure could be picked up for between £80 and £150, $110—360.

A set of Derby figures of the Continents. The presence of gilding on the bases dates these figures, original Derby creations, in the mid-1760's, though earlier examples exist.

An early Derby Chinoiserie group, probably modelled by Planché. Groups such as this, which display a remarkably mature use of porcelain as a material, are unfortunately rare.

137

museum and exhibition catalogues as such. The discovery of the difference caused a great depression in the price of the Derby figures of the middle period and affected to a certain extent those of the really early pieces. Today, however, the interest in early Chelsea and Bow is equalled by that in Derby of the same date though the number of pieces appearing on the market is rather limited. Even more restricted is the number of pieces from Longton Hall, Staffordshire's only porcelain factory in the early period. William Littler, a saltglaze potter, founded this factory in 1749. It was to become another vehicle for William Duesbury's decoration and he was to have a financial stake in the factory during its closing years and eventually took over some of its moulds.

The porcelain William Littler produced was fairly coarse. It contained a high proportion of soaprock and was extremely liable to crack during the firing. At the best it tends to have a greyish appearance and a soapy feel. The forms of the wares and the models for the figures take their inspiration from Meissen, or rather from Chelsea porcelain imitations of Meissen. In fact Littler did not stop at taking mere inspiration from Chelsea, but took moulds direct from figures and dishes made at the London factory. As a result of this process the pieces produced were slightly smaller than their Chelsea prototypes and the colouring rather less brilliant. Peculiar to the factory, and a distinctive feature of its production, is the cobalt blue used by Littler as a ground colour and called after him, Littler's blue. This is to be found on vases and tea wares.

Apart from the peony and other leaf dishes copied via Chelsea from Meissen, Longton Hall made a whole range of lettuce leaf moulded bowls,

Left

A pair of Derby groups of Musicians. These are rather finer than the average decorative groups of the mid-1760's. The flower encrusted gazebos in which the figures are sitting are unusual, and in fact not found with other subjects. The ignorance which has long surrounded Derby china is emphasized by the fact that these were illustrated before the last war as Bow, in the standard work on that factory.

This page

Left

A Longton Hall figure emblematic of Autumn, after a Chelsea original and from a set of the Seasons. The Chelsea figure is slightly larger and better modelled than this copy.

5 in. high.

Centre

A Longton Hall figure of a Musician after a Meissen original by J. J. Kändler.. A direct copy taken by a mould from the Meissen figure.

6 in. high.

Right

A Longton Hall figure of Columbine, also taken from a Meissen original.

5 in. high.

A Derby group of Children emblematic of the Seasons. Mock Meissen mark. This group, with its rocky grasswork base, is typical of the 1780's at Derby. The slightly fussier decoration, using a greater range of colours, is to be found at Meissen also during this period and looks forward to the 19th century. Groups of this date are sharing in the increased interest in the porcelain of the end of the century.

dishes, sauceboats, and other wares. These, and the strawberry leaf moulded pieces are among the factory's finest and most original productions. The strawberry leaf wares often also show the factory's decoration at its best, by the so-called 'The Trembly Rose' painter. It would be extremely hard today to form a collection of Longton Hall without ample financial means and much patience. However, in any collection which illustrates the influence of Meissen on the English porcelain factories, Longton Hall should feature prominently.

When the moulds from the Longton Hall factory were dispersed some of them were taken by William Duesbury. The remainder were bought up by William Cookworthy of Bristol at an auction in Salisbury in 1760. As a result several Longton Hall models of both figures and wares, particularly sauceboats, are to be found in a hardpaste porcelain, generally overfired. These are not 19th century fakes, but come from the first English hardpaste factories at Bristol and Plymouth. These two centres had a virtually simultaneous and indistinguishable production. The factory was originally established at Plymouth by William Cookworthy. He had been conducting experiments with china clay and feldspar as early as 1745 and started production in about 1765. At first his results were rather erratic, liable to firecracks and discolouration in the kiln. The successful pieces, however, are extremely fine. They include elaborate shell centre pieces such as were made earlier at Bow, Worcester and Derby, and mugs of bell shape painted with exotic birds. The painter of these is generally called Monsieur Soqui, as it is known that a decorator of that name was employed at the factory. He had previously been at Sèvres, the French soft paste factory. However, there is no concrete evidence to confirm this traditional attribution.

Richard Champion, who founded the Bristol factory in about 1770 had been associated with Cookworthy's experiments and actually bought his patent rights from him in 1774. He moved the Plymouth works to his own factory at this time, and was, compared with Cookworthy, a much more prolific potter. He had the services of two good modellers, Tebo, who had worked previously at Bow and Worcester, and Pierre Stephan, a Frenchman later employed at Derby. They produced for him some extremely attractive

139

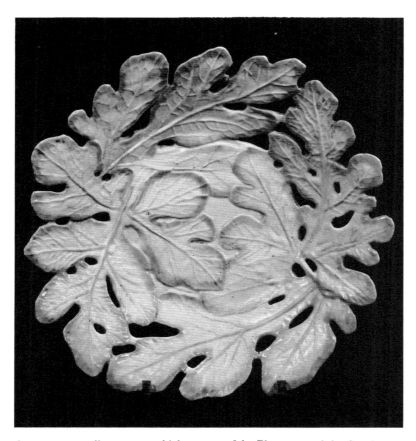

figures, outstanding among which are sets of the Elements and the Continents, such as were made at the majority of the soft paste factories. Complete sets of these, as with those from other sources, are very popular. Another very successful theme was represented by figures of children with animals. These, which are well modelled and coloured, suffer only from a tendency to collapse in the firing and to lean in directions not originally intended by their creator.

Champion also made magnificent hexagonal vases painted apparently by the same hand as the bell shaped mugs from Plymouth. These too suffered from a slight failure to hold their shape in the kiln.

This type of decoration does not extend to the table wares. They are more the vehicle for subjects in a neoclassical idiom. The contemporary decoration of Sèvres porcelain and the designs of the Adam family are echoed at Bristol by classical swags and medallions. The palette used is not brilliant, being dominated by greens and clarets with a certain amount of gilding. As at Worcester, armorial wares were produced, but these are not common. Many pieces of this type are marked in blue enamel with crossed batons, derived from the crossed swords of Meissen and often accompanied by numerals also in blue.

Interest in Plymouth and Bristol porcelain has varied over the years. The appeal tends to be greater in the West country where the china was made and where, indeed, the great majority of it is still to be found today. Collectors in the West of England are naturally attracted to these factories. In this way the market in Plymouth and Bristol resembles that in Lowestoft or in the South Wales factories, and today prices for rare examples may well prove higher locally than on the international market. If they do turn up in the salerooms, the competition generally develops between collectors from the area of origin.

The record price for a piece of Bristol porcelain was set in 1921 when £1,250, $3,000, was paid at auction for Jane Burke's teapot: in the previous year another, which had belonged to Edmund Burke, the orator, brought almost as much. These prices were extremely high, and equivalent sums have not been given for Bristol products since, nor indeed is it likely that the market will ever reach comparable heights again. The factory's most elaborate products, the hexagonal vases, many of which passed down through the Fry family, whose ancestor was in partnership with Champion, are not greatly esteemed today. This is fairly surprising, since these are among the finest of Champion's works; but their fate is shared almost universally by the large vases of Worcester and Chelsea as we have seen.

Equally, the table wares are little competed for. This is partly the result of their comparatively uniform appearance, which contrasts with the variety of the wares of Chelsea, Worcester and Bow. The figures, however, though uncommon, are varied and often of fine quality, when successfully fired. The models present an interesting difference from the Meissen inspired creations of the soft paste factories.

Like Longton Hall or Lowestoft, Bristol is not in constant supply. Unless he lives in the West of England the collector who wishes to acquire specimens will need patience or good luck to form a collection of any size or representative nature. The factories at Bristol and Plymouth, in short, form an unusual enclave in the soft paste world of English 18th century porcelain. Perhaps as a result, they are not the objects of such general interest as the soft paste centres. They fall rather after the early period, and yet do not share the later decorative styles which are the subject of the next chapter. Of all the English factories they offer the least promising prospect.

A Bow mug painted with the quail pattern found at most of the English factories as well as Chantilly and Meissen. The shape is typical of Bow and quite different from the Worcester bell shaped mug.
This recently sold for £126, $300, which shows that Bow wares have still plenty of room to appreciate.

THE LATER FACTORIES

A Worcester jardinière painted with shells by Thomas Baxter, Flight & Barr factory, *circa* 1805. An example of Baxter's famous shell painting. It is most commonly found, as in this example, with a salmon ground. A plate with this decoration today is worth about £125, $300. More elaborate pieces such as this vase are worth correspondingly more.

The 1780's saw the end of the great early porcelain factories in London. This coincided with the waning of the rococo style which throughout Europe was the underlying impetus and inspiration of the best porcelain manufacturers. At Worcester the original partnership was succeeded by two factories run by the Flight and Barr families and by Chamberlains. The factory at Derby continued, as we have seen, to produce much the same figures as in earlier decades, but in a somewhat less attractive style of decoration. Their wares, like those of Worcester, consisted in the main in large dinner and dessert services, vases, inkwells, jardinières and little decorative pieces. A factory near Derby at Pinxton was founded by Billingsley in 1796 while Josiah Spode began to produce fine porcelain at Stoke-on-Trent in about 1790. In about 1795 John Rose began production at Coalport in Shropshire. The hardpaste factory at Bristol was succeeded by the Newhall factory at Hanley in 1781, and this specialised in the production of teawares, generally with decoration of Chinese inspiration. Wales, which hitherto had only produced pottery— at Swansea—joined the porcelain producing fraternity with two factories at Swansea and Nantgarw where Billingsley once again was involved. The last serious factory to enter the field of porcelain production was Brameld's at Rockingham which added porcelain to pottery in around 1826.

Compared with the early pioneering factories all these later establishments were long classed as makers of decorative rather than collectors' pieces. However, the high prices attained by the pieces of the early period have forced many would-be collectors to focus their attention on this age of technical expertise and almost faultless decoration. The economic necessity has been accompanied by a great burst of scholastic activity which has greatly increased our knowledge of the management of these factories and the artists who worked in them. Several of them, as in the earlier period and on the continent, were employed at more than one factory. William Billingsley, who worked at Derby, Nantgarw and Swansea as a decorator also managed the factory at Pinxton and at least one decorating shop of his own at Mansfield for three years around the turn of the century. He is typical of his period and it is in terms of such outstanding decorators that the age is best viewed.

Attention to the decoration is particularly important since the forms, in a neoclassical era which appreciated simplicity of line, were generally much plainer than those of the mid 18th century, and were also much more rigidly standardised than earlier pieces. Vases tend to be much the same shape, generally the campana form of those illustrated. Naturally there are variations in the handles, the mouldings of the rims and in the proportions from one factory to the next; but it is the decoration which distinguishes the productions of one factory from another and the good piece from the ordinary.

At Derby we know the names of several decorators apart from Billingsley, and can link them with specific types of decoration. Flower painting was done by Complin, 'Quaker' Pegg and Steele. Complin specialised in painting

Three Derby vases painted with hunting scenes—iron red crowned crossed batons and D marks. The shape is an absolutely standard one in the Regency period. Here the handles are formed as snakes, though they are sometimes formed as acanthus leaves. It is the decoration that distinguishes these from their contemporaries, since these hunting scenes are far more exciting than standard floral or formal subjects unless these are of unusually fine quality.

146

Derby porcelain plaque, probably painted by 'Quaker' Pegg, of whom the fully blown flower is typical. Similar, but tighter arrangements of flowers are to be found by Steele. This type of decoration also occurs on vases and plates.

flowers and fruit almost in a miniature technique. Pegg's style was altogether more opulent and generous: his flowers are richly coloured and full blown. Steele, who also worked at Rockingham later on, painted bunches of flowers and fruit on ledges. The finest examples of his painting are generally plaques, such as the one illustrated. His manner of painting grapes is very distinctive. Services with botanical specimens, named on the reverse, were another of the factory's successful lines. The best of these have yellow borders, though they are more commonly found with pale blue and salmon pink borders. The decoration of these is associated with Brewer. Numerous pieces were decorated with landscape scenes by the Lucases, father and son, while Robertson produced pieces decorated with shipping subjects. These, too, often have their titles painted on the reverse.

The best decoration on Worcester was done by Thomas Baxter in London, who, unusually among decorators, had the habit of signing, and even dating, pieces he painted. He was particularly renowned for his shell painting, as on the sauce tureen illustrated. He also produced services painted with different feathers. These were of course, not the only types of decoration he produced, the jardinière shown illustrates his painting in the neoclassical idiom not unlike that of Angelica Kauffmann. The tradition of coloured grounds, so successfully established in the first period, died hard at Worcester. The colours change slightly. Claret and a limey apple green predominate, though salmon pink is also popular and occurs on wares painted with shells or botanical specimens. Royal blue grounds are more common at this time at Coalport or Derby than at either of the Worcester factories. The coloured

grounds at both Chamberlain's and the Flight & Barr factories are frequently found with very fine landscape painting, often of named views among which Worcester and its surroundings predominate. Both here and at Derby the influence of contemporary prints and paintings is to be seen on wares of this type.

The Pinxton factory is, despite the considerable amount of research devoted to it, still fairly difficult to assess with confidence. As a result, many attributions to it are, to say the least, dubious and the collector who is offered pieces ascribed to this very rare factory should proceed with caution. Comparatively few of its products were marked, though pieces do exist with the name Pinxton in full, or the letter P in script before a pattern number. Sufficient of these are known to make certain the attribution of some forms to the factory. The shape of the cream jug, with its dented handle, is particularly distinctive, whilst the sugar basin, though conforming generally to the type made at Worcester and Newhall at this date, shows subtle differences in the shape of the handles and the curve of the body. The scope of the factory was fairly limited and its products probably only included tea and flatwares, beakers, jardinières and small vases in imitation of Derby.

Rose's factory at Coalport or Coalbrookdale was the successor of the Caughley works. Many of its products, like the service illustrated, adhered closely to the type obtaining generally at this time. The central panels contain finely painted and varied subjects, the coloured borders are enriched with gilding. The wares of this type were only one aspect of the factory's production. More usual and more peculiar to Coalport are the flower encrusted wares which at their best can be superb. The baskets and vases of this type are fairly common, but dishes and leaves containing flowers and fruit are rare and desirable.

Josiah Spode's porcelain was the product of a great technician. The forms he used were very simple indeed. His vases were of beaker shape or with plain loop handles to the shoulders. The wares were similarly plain and adhered to the standard shapes of the day, but the decoration raised his wares above the level of many contemporary products. Even pieces in the red, blue and gold patterns of Oriental flowers which were the stock in trade of all the porcelain manufacturers at the time were more brilliant and distinguished when interpreted by Spode's painters. Pieces of all types were made by Spode

Pair of Worcester jardinières and stands decorated by Thomas Baxter, signed and dated 1804. The artist's signature appears in the lower right hand corner of the panel on the left hand vase. The classical scrolls are in colours on pale yellow grounds. The borders show typical gilding of this period. Baxter worked on Worcester and Welsh porcelains.

with decoration of this form. Much more desirable though, and harder to find, are pieces with naturalistic floral decoration. Many of the pieces of the best period of Spode's production bear the mark 'SPODE' accompanied by the pattern number.

In the eyes of many collectors today, particularly those in Wales or with Welsh connections, the products of the two short-lived Glamorgan factories are appreciated more than their English contemporaries. This is caused by a variety of factors. Firstly, Welsh ceramics are very limited in number, the porcelains of Nantgarw and Swansea and the earlier Swansea pottery being all that serious collectors consider. Secondly, the wares which these two factories produced were of outstanding quality. The paste was extremely fine and translucent at Nantgarw, while that of Swansea, though less brilliant, lent itself to very thin potting. The quality of the ware was combined with a high level of decoration carried out at both factories by such as Thomas Pardoe, Moses Webster, Henry Morris, William Billingsley and others. A certain amount of Nantgarw wares were sent to London for decoration there. As always at this date, the majority of the pieces have floral decoration. A great proportion of this takes the form of simple bunches of flowers, while a finer and less common type has sprays of a botanical type. At Swansea pieces were produced with decoration in red, blue and gold in the Oriental style. Also from Swansea are to be found wares in the *famille rose* manner such as the very rare specimen illustrated. Nantgarw produced wares with coloured borders or grounds, plates in imitation of early Meissen porcelain, pieces with central subject panels and, as in the case of Worcester, the most sought after pieces decorated with birds. Of these the highest level is represented by the Mackintosh service, executed for The Mackintosh of Mackintosh in the Highlands of Scotland, each piece with a different bird at the centre.

Six pieces of Swansea porcelain, mainly decorated by Henry Morris. These show a variety of the shapes used at the factory.

One feature of the Welsh factories which is slightly limiting and which caused the focussing of interest on the differing types of decoration is the comparatively small range of shapes. Indeed 'form' pieces are in an unusually small minority in the productions of both factories. At Nantgarw this is perhaps even more marked than at Swansea. Both factories produced dessert wares and teasets with the accompanying icepails, sauce tureens, tazzas, shaped dishes, teapots, jugs, bowls and sugar basins. At Swansea, vases were also made. At Nantgarw only the flat wares, i.e. the plates and dishes were marked. Generally the mark was the word NANT-GARW impressed with the letters C.W., which stand for 'China Works'. Occasionally the mark is painted in underglaze blue. At Swansea marks were used more generally on pieces of all shapes. On the flat wares impressed marks occur, sometimes with the word SWANSEA accompanied by a single trident or by two crossed tridents. On flat pieces and on shaped specimens there also occurs a red stencil mark with the word in block capitals. This mark, or a close imitation of it, was used on Coalport porcelains after the Swansea factory was shut down. It should be viewed with suspicion unless it appears on a piece that is undoubtedly a Swansea shape. Almost all the known shapes and patterns at Swansea and Nantgarw are recorded by W. D. John in his two

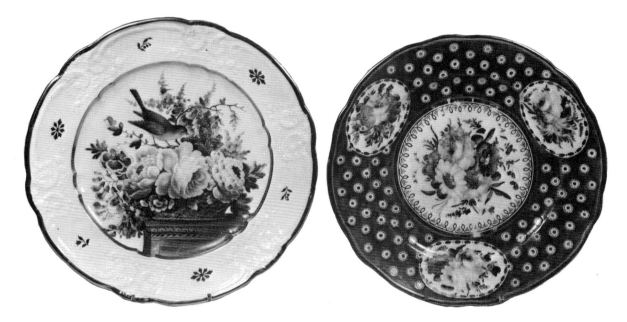

monographs on the factories. No one should embark on the collection of Welsh porcelain without reference to these.

Owing to extremely keen competition among collectors in the late 1950's, certain types of Nantgarw and Swansea porcelain fetched prices which they have barely held in recent years. The Mackintosh service in particular has suffered in this respect. The lower strata, the ordinary good quality wares which are less affected by the whims of a few collectors and more by the interest of the average buying public, have continued a steady upward trend which shows no signs of dimishing. This buoyancy is occasionally helped along by the discovery of some unknown pattern or shape, which creates a fresh, though temporary, centre of interest.

Just as national or local interest has contributed much to the steady demand and appreciation for Welsh porcelain, so wares from Rockingham in the North of England, a comparatively late factory, have benefited from local interest and are in increasing demand today. The manufacture of porcelain here sprang out of an already established pottery just as that at Swansea. Stylistically the productions of this factory adhere to the taste of the reign of William IV. They are more elaborate in form than the wares of the opening years of the

Two Nantgarw plates—impressed Nant-Garw C.W. marks:
left: painted with flowers and a bird on a ledge by William Pollard. The border moulded with scrolls and the extremely clear paste are typical of this factory.
right: with turquoise ground from the Duke of Cambridge service a rich interpretation of the Sèvres style of decoration.
Both these pieces come from the top end of the scale in Nant-Garw production and are of the type that has not appreciated as much in value as the lesser pieces.

A frame of four Minton *pâte-sur-pâte* plaques by L. Solon. These pieces, each signed with the artist's initials are small examples of the work Solon did on large vases for Mintons. These were originally very expensive to produce and sold for high prices. Today they are still expensive, but have not shown a good appreciation in value.

century. The decoration is generally floral, though birds and named landscapes also feature on some of the finer pieces. The greater proportion of the production consists of tablewares, though vases, butterfly shaped boxes, scent bottles encrusted with flowers, and a small number of figures and animals were also made. Many of those pieces are marked with a griffin above the word 'Brameld', either in iron red or puce. Specimens bearing these marks are generally more valuable than unmarked examples, and no piece without the mark should be accepted as Rockingham unless the shape can be found in an authoritative work on the subject.

Until recently the United States duty on pieces made since 1832 placed all more recent productions at a disadvantage in the market and discouraged collectors from exploring the porcelains of the Victorian era with much enthusiasm. However, this restriction has now been removed from pieces over one hundred years old, and so the outlook on wares made during the intervening period has altered. This change covers, among other salient events, the Great Exhibition of 1851 and the Paris Exhibition of 1862. These generated the production of particularly showy pieces often displaying more magnificence and imitative skill than originality. Many Minton and Royal Worcester vases in imitation of 18th century Sèvres of the more elaborate sort date from this period. So too do the pieces decorated in white slip by Thomas Bott. These were technically quite original, but the subjects were extremely derivative, often being taken from Vandyke or some other Old Master. However, the most successful exponent of decoration in white slip or *pâte-sur-pâte* was L. Solon who came from Sèvres to Minton in 1862 and during the next 40 years produced a series of vases and plaques in the technique which are leading examples of the Art Nouveau style. His son, M. L. Solon also produced plaques in advanced techniques and using acid etching and other methods. Like the contemporary cameo glass these *pâte-sur-pâte* wares were very expensive to produce. Therefore they were originally costly. Though today they fetch considerable prices these represent comparatively small increases in proportion to the original cost of the pieces.

The majority of the elaborate showpieces which date from the Victorian era have in fact risen little in price, if at all. Any family still possessing pieces of this type acquired during the course of the last century would probably make a loss if they were to dispose of them today. On the other hand a collector acquiring wares of this sort today should find a good appreciation in their value in the future; though it is unlikely to equal that of the finer productions from the beginning of the century. For these combine the dignity of being old-established antiques with high quality and excellent decoration.

The value of pieces of this period is less subject to the vagaries of taste and

Pinxton pieces from a tea service. This shows the peculiar shape of the jug and the forms of the teapot and sugar basin and teapot and stand. This particular service was unmarked but specimens sometimes are marked with a P followed by a number. This service was painted in a remarkable combination of yellow and purple.

fashion than those of the earlier generation. Their appeal is more widely based and therefore they have tended to appreciate steadily and should certainly continue to do so. The productions of Flight, Barr & Barr are the classic examples of this: they are of very consistent quality and, the pieces decorated by Baxter apart, are within the reach of most collectors. Shell and feather decorated specimens on the other hand are the subject of tremendous competition at present. Whether this phenomenon will continue, one cannot tell.

The demand for the more exceptional specimens from Swansea and Nantgarw has not shown much change in the last decade. The Mackintosh service has, if anything, depreciated slightly. The lesser pieces of average or fairly good standard have gained in value to some extent; but it does seem that there are only a few collectors prepared to spend more than about £200, $500, on a single piece. This apparent ceiling will no doubt eventually disappear, expecially as the prices of the less remarkable pieces increase. Despite this, the wise collector should still concentrate on rarer pieces with unusual or fine quality decoration. This rule applies too to the other contemporary factories. All these are attractive, from the investor's point of view, by virtue of the low base price at which the beginner can pick up pieces which are good, if small, a situation which contrasts with that confronting the collector of 18th century porcelain. How long this built-in advantage will endure is questionable; but the succeeding age, alas, produced little to attract the attention of the collector of fine porcelain.

POTTERY & PORCELAIN AS AN INVESTMENT

Today the more important pieces that appear on the international art market tend to be syphoned off into public collections in Britain, Australia, and North America. This reduces the amount of really good pieces left in general circulation and causes their market value to increase. At the same time the number of would-be collectors increases daily. So the future promises fairly well. The problem then is to choose which pieces, or the products of which factory are liable to appreciate faster than others, or which have been recently neglected. One must also judge which of those types that are presently in vogue are popular for good reasons and which are liable to prove the objects of short-lived enthusiasm. Perhaps the classic example of current neglect, in contrast, as we have seen, to a popularity that was out of proportion half a century or more ago, is found in the Chelsea wares of the Gold Anchor Period. Even here though, there are small signs of a recovery in interest, though it would be foolish ever to expect prices such as were paid in the past for pieces of this type.

Blue and white porcelain and delftwares of the 18th century, fields that have only lately attracted attention, seem set firmly on an appreciating trend. The inherent quality of these pieces, for long unacknowledged, has now given them a secure niche on collectors' shelves. They should surely maintain their interest. These two categories have the advantage over some of the other types which are available but are both much more expensive to acquire and yet will not increase in value any more quickly. However, they are unlikely to show any surprising changes in value.

The increase in value is only one reward of the investment. Intangible it may be, but the pleasure of possession provided by good pieces is not to be discounted. In fact a collection formed solely on the basis of personal taste is by far the most likely to prove the best financial investment.

It would be wrong to think that any china one buys must increase steadily in value unless certain rules are rigidly observed. The collector should try to acquire as much knowledge as possible about whatever type he intends to acquire. This is not to be found in books, but can only be got with frequent examination of pieces. The public collections give the opportunity of seeing a wide panorama of specimens. Unfortunately it is generally not possible to touch the exhibits, so although the forms and colours of the various factories may be studied, the feel of the pieces is lost. This is in many ways the most important criterion, the lack of which can be limiting. One should be familiar with the weight, glaze and feel of the basic types. The only place where the opportunity does arise for close examination of specimens is the saleroom. In London there are frequent sales at either Christie's, Sotheby's or Puttick & Simpson. Here pieces of all sorts may be examined, varying in quality and condition. At the sale itself, the prices fetched can be noted. For those who cannot actually attend sales it is well worth while subscribing to receive the price lists which are later published.

In every sale there are many pieces which are chipped or otherwise damaged. Some may well have been repaired almost invisibly: today it is possible to repair pieces so as to deceive all but the most experienced eyes. Some repairs in fact can only be detected by long exposure to ultraviolet rays, though transmitted light may well reveal any cracks or breaks in flat wares, mugs, tea and coffee pots. The best policy to pursue is not to have anything to do with repaired pieces, though of course the extent of the repair may well not be serious. If on a figure the hands have been slightly restored, and it is an otherwise rare piece, it is worth having. If on the other hand the head has been broken off, it is best left well alone.

The most successful collectors, from all points of view, are uncompromising. They buy only those pieces which are as good, if not better, than the pieces they already have. Even if a piece turns up which they do not have, and its condition is not all that it might be, unless it is almost unique, they leave it well alone. This is the safest policy. One perfect piece may well cost as much as three damaged ones, but the eventual satisfaction will well outweigh the difference. No piece should be bought which does not appeal directly to the collector. If you do not like a piece you are offered, do not buy it; there is probably some good reason for the dislike which possession would reveal only too soon.

Collecting is intensely personal. Pieces affect, and are affected by their possessors. This is why collectors are always keen to acquire specimens that have previously been in famous collections. It is almost as though each owner imparted a small part of his personality to each object.

No collection of any merit is formed without a great deal of hard work, discipline and knowledge. It will not be made overnight. But of one thing you can be sure, it will afford enjoyment that, all financial gain apart, makes collecting English Pottery and Porcelain a very good investment.

INDEX